Achieving ISO/IEC 20000
Finance for service managers

The 'Achieving ISO/IEC 20000' series

This publication is the fifth in a series of ten publications related to ISO/IEC 20000. Each publication provides advice on different aspects of ISO/IEC 20000. The books in the 'Achieving ISO/IEC 20000' series are:

Management decisions and documentation (BIP 0030)

Why people matter (BIP 0031)

Making metrics work (BIP 0032)

Managing end-to-end service (BIP 0033)

Finance for service managers (BIP 0034)

Enabling change (BIP 0035)

Keeping the service going (BIP 0036)

Capacity management (BIP 0037)

Integrated service management (BIP 0038)

The differences between BS 15000 and ISO/IEC 20000 (BIP 0039)

This series provides practical guidance and advice on introducing IT service management best practice in accordance with ISO/IEC 20000. More details on the content of each publication are given in *Books in the 'Achieving ISO/IEC 20000' series*, at the end of this book.

Although security issues are covered in ISO/IEC 20000, the 'Achieving ISO/IEC 20000' series does not cover security requirements. Information on security can be found in the BSI publications that are listed in the *Bibliography* in Appendix B.

Other publications

BSI also publishes:

A managers' guide to service management (BIP 0005) is intended for managers who are new to support services or who are faced with major changes to their existing support facility. This book takes the form of informative explanations, guidance and recommendations.

IT service management – Self-assessment workbook (BIP 0015) is an easy to use checklist that complements ISO/IEC 20000 and is designed to assist an organization's internal assessment of their services and the extent to which they conform to the specified requirements in ISO/IEC 20000.

Achieving ISO/IEC 20000
Finance for service managers

Dr Jenny Dugmore and Shirley Lacy

Business
Information

First published in the UK in 2005

Second edition published in the UK in 2006

by
BSI
389 Chiswick High Road
London W4 4AL

Typeset in Frutiger by Typobatics Limited
Printed in Great Britain by Formara Limited

British Library Cataloguing in Publication Data
A catalogue record for this book is available from the British Library

ISBN 0-580-47462-3

Contents

Foreword 1

Acknowledgements 3

Introduction 5

What is ISO/IEC 20000? 5

The purpose of ISO/IEC 20000 5

The 'Achieving ISO/IEC 20000' series 6

Additional advice 6

Chapter 1 – Financial matters 9

Finance and ISO/IEC 20000 9

ISO/IEC 20000 requirements (ISO/IEC 20000-1, 6.4) 10

Service provider governance 11

Chapter 2 – Financial terms and definitions 13

Introduction 13

Capital and revenue/operating costs 13

Capital cost 13

Revenue operating costs 15

Fixed and variable costs 16

Direct and indirect costs 16

Balance sheet 17

Chapter 3 – Policy, process and procedures 19

Introduction 19

Why policy, process and procedure? 19

Organization-wide policies 21
Policies required by ISO/IEC 20000-1 23
Policies recommended by ISO/IEC 20000-2 24
Chapter 4 – Planning for effective financial control **25**
Introduction 25
Cost models and cost types 26
Detailing the costs 29
Apportioning and allocating costs 36
Using a cost model 39
Chapter 5 – Budgeting and accounting processes **41**
Introduction 41
Establishing a budget 41
Monitoring and reporting costs 43
Budget variance and risk management 44
Chapter 6 – Financial responsibilities **47**
Introduction 47
ISO/IEC 20000 and management commitment 47
Who does financial management? 49
Financial control and authorization levels 50
Chapter 7 – Charging **51**
Introduction 51
ISO/IEC 20000-2 recommendations 51
Impact of charging 52
Basis for charging 54
Pricing 55
Differences between commercial and in-house service providers 57
Chapter 8 – The Plan-Do-Check-Act (PDCA) cycle **59**
Introduction 59
The cost of services 59

Finance and the PDCA cycle 59

Chapter 9 – Interfaces to other service management processes **61**

Introduction 61

Implications for integrated service management 61

Relationships to other service management processes 62

Chapter 10 – Example metrics and audit evidence **63**

Chapter 11 – Regulatory and legal compliance **65**

Introduction 65

Example regulatory compliance requirements 66

Appendix A – ISO/IEC 20000 requirements in summary **69**

Appendix B – Bibliography and further references **77**

Books in the 'Achieving ISO/IEC 20000' series **79**

Foreword

Financial management is central to any successful service provider, irrespective of whether they charge for their services or are funded out of what is considered to be a financial ‘black hole’. The importance of value for money and understanding of true cost of ownership continue to increase in importance, with senior management being challenged on these aspects of their service. Often it is the responsibility of the service provider to prove they represent value for money, in some cases this is tested by the customers themselves.

Commercial and in-house service providers are both under these pressures, with customers changing from one service provider to another if they believe there is an advantage to them to do so. Customer satisfaction is also strongly influenced by value for money although this may be based on perceptions in the absence of the information required to make an objective judgment. Financial information and effective processes are particularly important in business relationships, service level management and supplier management

Some service managers view budgeting and accounting as an alien activity, outside their normal scope and involving a strange language. However, financial management is part of the professional management of any function. There are also many parallels between budgeting and accounting and other service management processes, such as service level management. For example, a budget, which is a set of financial targets, plays the same part in the financial management process as service targets in service level management. Similarly, a meeting to discuss the differences between actual costs and budgeted costs is similar to a service review comparing actual service levels and service targets performed under service level management. Both processes provide input to a plan for improving the service.

Finally, effective service management requires financial management competence, particularly among the process owners, but it does not require accountancy training.

Dr Jenny Dugmore

Acknowledgements

This book has been produced with the input and assistance of people involved in the practical aspects of delivering services across all sectors. We would like to thank them for sharing their views and providing constructive criticism, case studies and practical techniques.

It is not possible to list all of those who have helped, but particular thanks goes to: Alison Holt of Synergy International Ltd; Barbara Eastman; Bob Thomas; Borge Ellgaard; Clive Strawford of More and More Investments Limited; Hella Schrader of Financial Times; Ian Whyte of Bishops Beech; Ivor Evans of DIYmonde Solutions Inc; James Finister; James Mullock of Osborne Clarke; John Groom of West Groom Consulting; Les Tabernacle of Pilkington Plc; Lynda Cooper of Fox IT; Madeline Gunner; Martin Jackson; Norman Yap of Siemens Business Services; Penny Jeffreys; Peter Lickiss; Sharon Hampton of Serco Solutions Ltd; and Tony Jenkins of DOMAINetc.

Finally, we would like to thank Simone Levy and Kieran Parkinson of BSI for their support, helpful suggestions, tact and patience during the production of the 'Achieving ISO/IEC 20000' series.

INTRODUCTION

What is ISO/IEC 20000?

ISO/IEC 20000 is the first IT service management process standard to be produced by the International Organization for Standardization (ISO), and it is based on the knowledge and experience gained by experts working in the field.

ISO/IEC 20000 was produced by Technical Committee ISO/IEC JTC 1/SC 7, *Software and system engineering*, and was based on BS 15000, which was produced by BSI Technical Committee BDD/3, *Information services management*.

ISO/IEC 20000 is in two parts.

- ISO/IEC 20000-1 is a specification containing requirements that must be met in order to achieve ISO/IEC 20000.
- ISO/IEC 20000-2 is a code of practice on how to achieve the requirements in ISO/IEC 20000-1.

The requirements in Part 1 (i.e. ISO/IEC 20000-1) are applicable to service providers of all sizes and types, regardless of whether the organization is public or private sector, internal or external. The recommendations in Part 2 (i.e. ISO/IEC 20000-2) are optional approaches to achieving the requirements in Part 1. Although optional, the recommendations are also practical and proven methods that are normally appropriate.

The purpose of ISO/IEC 20000

ISO/IEC 20000 provides the basis for assessing whether service providers have best practice, reliable, repeatable and measurable processes applied consistently across their organization. As a process-based standard the requirements are independent of organizational structure or of the tools used to automate the service management processes. ISO/IEC 20000-1 provides the basis for formal certification schemes and other audits.

The 'Achieving ISO/IEC 20000' series

The `Achieving ISO/IEC 20000' series is designed to explain the requirements of ISO/IEC 20000. An abstract of the ISO/IEC 20000 clauses that are most relevant to the topic of financial management is given in Appendix A. Also, Table 1 provides a clause-by-clause guide to the content of each of the books in the `Achieving ISO/IEC 20000' series.

This fifth publication in the `Achieving ISO/IEC 20000' series describes the requirements for the financial processes given in ISO/IEC 20000-1, 6.4. As with other publications in this series, the supporting recommendations given in ISO/IEC 20000-2 are also described.

In ISO/IEC 20000, emphasis has been placed on the importance of a service provider understanding the costs of the service they deliver and how the financial processes interface with other management processes. This publication includes case studies, examples and other information on financial processes and their use by a service provider aiming to achieve ISO/IEC 20000.

Additional advice

Service providers aiming to achieve ISO/IEC 20000 may find it useful to seek advice on best practice, the qualifications available for individual service management professionals and ISO/IEC 20000 certification. Details of these can be found via the web pages cited in Appendix B.

Table 1 – Clause-by-clause guide to the 'Achieving ISO/IEC 20000' series

ISO/IEC 20000 clause	BIP 0030	BIP 0031	BIP 0032	BIP 0033	BIP 0034	BIP 0035	BIP 0036	BIP 0037	BIP 0038	BIP 0039
Terms and definitions	■									■
Management responsibility	■								■	■
Documentation requirements	■									■
Competence, awareness and training		■								■
Planning and implementing service management									■	■
Plan – Do – Check – Act cycle									■	■
Planning and implementing new or changed services									■	■
Service level management				■						■
Service reporting			■							■
Service continuity and availability management							■			■
Budgeting and accounting for IT services					■					■
Information security management	See BSI publications on information security management in the BIP 0070 series									■
Capacity management								■		■
Business relationship management				■						■
Supplier management				■						■
Incident management							■			■
Problem management							■			■
Configuration management						■				■
Change management						■				■
Release management						■				■

CHAPTER 1

Financial matters

Finance and ISO/IEC 20000

Money matters to all organizations. Any organization that does not understand and manage its costs is badly managed, regardless of how well it may otherwise perform. Value for money, perceived or real, can have a huge impact on the customer's satisfaction with a service. It can have a large impact on the ability of a service provider to ensure that investment in the service is agreed.

Financial processes are an important part of service management. The requirements for budgeting and accounting included in ISO/IEC 20000 relate to management accounting and do not require accountancy qualifications. However, service managers need to have some understanding of how budgets are produced and how actual costs are tracked against a budget.

Definition: Budgeting and accounting

Budgeting is the process by which a business develops a set of financial targets. The budgeting process allows evaluation of performance against the service provider's financial goals, from tracking of actual costs against budgeted costs, giving control over the spending of money. Agreeing the budget takes into account the previous year's actual costs, predicted changes and an understanding of what is needed to manage services within budget.

Accounting is the process by which financial information about a service provider is recorded, classified, reported, analysed and interpreted by the service provider as part of the control and tracking of costs. In service management this provides information on costs by service, by process or by customer.

A service provider will not achieve the standards required by ISO/IEC 20000 if financial management is considered to be only 'something the accountants do'. Service managers also need enough understanding of financial information to demonstrate that they manage the costs of a service effectively. The process owner for the financial processes is particularly important in this aspect of ISO/IEC 20000 requirements. The role of the process owner is described in BIP 0031, *Why people matter*.

Every process incurs costs and most service providers seek to minimize costs, usually by improving efficiency. Aiming for the standards required to achieve ISO/IEC 20000 brings the benefits of improved financial management processes. These benefits include:

- increased confidence in budgets and predictability of finances;
- accurate cost information to support investment decisions;
- provision of a firm baseline of cost of services from which to measure improvements;
- a basis for judging value for money and improving value for money from informed decisions on service and process improvements;
- charges, where applied, are understood, considered fair and therefore more acceptable;
- an increased competitive edge for commercial organizations.

The topics covered in this publication also include the role of financial information in the Plan-Do-Check-Act (PDCA) cycle, as described in Chapter 8. The relationship between financial processes and other service management processes, such as service reporting, business relationship management and the integration of individual processes, is described in Chapter 9 and in BIP 0038, *Integrated service management.*

Examples of metrics and illustrative audit evidence for financial processes are given in Chapter 10.

ISO/IEC 20000 requirements (ISO/IEC 20000-1, 6.4)

The requirements for budgeting and accounting are described in more detail in Chapter 5. One of the prime reasons for inclusion of budgeting and accounting in ISO/IEC 20000 is to ensure a service provider has effective control over costs and value for money and that the service provider's decision-making is based on good financial information as well as service information. This normally also involves the PDCA cycle and the other service management processes.

Control and authority

Management commitment and control is important for any aspect of service management, but there are specific requirements and recommendations for financial processes that support service management, as described in Chapter 6. These also provide part of the control that reduces the risk of fraud.

Charging

The requirements in ISO/IEC 20000-1, 6.4 relate to budgeting and accounting for IT services. In practice, all commercial service providers and many internal service providers have implemented some form of charging for the services they deliver. Despite being common practice, charging was not specified as a requirement in ISO/IEC 20000 because charging is not appropriate for some organizations. This is mainly when the overhead of charging will outweigh the benefits obtained. For example, a small service provider with a single group of in-house users may get the benefits of financial management processes from effective budgeting and accounting, and avoid the overhead of charging.

There are some recommendations on charging for any service provider that does charge for services, as described in Chapter 7.

Service provider governance

Budgeting and accounting processes are a fundamental business requirement for all organizations. The processes are part of an overall system of controls for regulatory and legal compliance that ensure the service provider's organization is operating with financial probity. The need for this system of controls for regulatory compliance directly affects service management processes.

This requirement for regulatory compliance is separate from the requirements of ISO/IEC 20000. However, service management processes are used to provide and demonstrate part of the compliance with regulatory and legal requirements. Examples of regulatory compliance requirements include Sarbanes-Oxley and Basel 2/Second Basel Accord, as described in Chapter 11.

Many organizations are required to deliver proof that they are providing value for money and their financial processes are included as part of this.

ISO/IEC 20000 provides support for this by ensuring processes are best practice and that financial information is available so that cost management and value for money initiatives are on a sound basis.

CHAPTER 2

Financial terms and definitions

Introduction

In service management discussions on issues such as the cost of the service, investment in new services or technology or during production of a new budget, accountancy terms may be used that refer to topics outside the scope of ISO/IEC 20000. Many of these relate to profit and loss/balance sheet accounting, whereas ISO/IEC 20000 is aligned to management accounting. However, service and financial discussions and the ISO/IEC 20000 requirements may be more easily understood by service managers if they also understand some basic accounting terms. This chapter does not cover all such terms, but those that are most relevant to service managers are outlined below. Any reader with background in accounting will find all these terms familiar and will not need to refer to the definitions and explanations provided.

Capital and revenue/operating costs

Two import classifications are capital and revenue costs. Revenue costs are also frequently referred to as operating costs. These costs must be identifiable as separate types in budgets. Financial processes handle capital and revenue costs separately.

Capital cost

Capital costs represent an investment that can be spread over the expected useful working life of the investment. They are items that could be re-sold if a service provider chooses to do so. The cost is recorded as an asset (defined below). These are usually one-off fixed costs depreciated (also defined below) over more than one accounting period.

There is a distinction between accounting for capital expenditure (as it appears on a profit and loss account) and accounting for the use of capital assets (as it appears on a balance sheet). This distinction is normally outside the scope of ISO/IEC 20000.

Assets

Capital assets have a cash value and come off a capital budget. The service provider's balance sheet shows capital assets and their depreciation. Capital assets may be bought. Some leasing arrangements allow for the leased item to be owned by the service provider at the end of the leasing period. IT assets are typically 'things that have been bought', but may include 'things that have been built'. Fixed assets are tangible property such as buildings, mainframes, PCs, printers, furniture and equipment.

Assets may include items such as service management monitoring systems, i.e. assets that are used in service management processes, or produced by service management processes. Some service providers also have intellectual property assets, e.g. specialist software developed by the service provider that has a value in financial terms.

Depreciation

This is the term used to describe the change in the value of a capital asset starting from its value when new to its residual value at the end of its predicted useful working life. A fully depreciated asset may have a book value of zero but may still be a useful part of an overall service. The reverse may be the case, the asset may no longer be usable but still have a value in the accounts. Depreciation spreads the cost of an investment over the expected useful working life and goes onto a balance sheet. It is important that the manager using the information in the budget and financial records understands if an entry is the total value of the item or the value for that budget year based on the rate of depreciation.

Assets still in use at the end of their predicted working life are referred to as being 'fully depreciated'. Assets that fail before the end of their predicted working life may remain in the accounts until they are fully depreciated. Alternatively, an accounting adjustment may be made. There are several methods of depreciation. For example, 'straight-line depreciation' allocates an equal reduction in value for each year of the asset's useful life. A PC 'depreciated over three years' would be recorded in the accounts as losing a third of its initial value each year, and at the end of three years the accounts would show it as having zero financial value.

Many different kinds of assets can be depreciated, such as machinery, buildings, furniture and equipment. To merit the additional step of being depreciated the asset must:

- have a useful life that can be predicted (and subsequently recorded);
- have a useful life of more than one financial year[1];
- wear out, decay, get used up, become obsolete or lose value in some other way.

Service managers involved in setting budgets also need to understand depreciation and how it affects the budget entries, as there is normally a need to make provisions for the actual replacement of major assets, and the cost needs to be allowed for when budgeting. Finance departments will give guidance on the method of depreciation to be employed. Depreciation rules are fixed for a whole organization, even if only one department in a large organization uses a particular type of depreciated asset.

Revenue/operating costs

Items funded out of revenue may represent a major expenditure, and may also represent a sizeable benefit to the service provider. However, revenue costs are purchases that are not subsequently available for re-sale by the service provider and a revenue cost must be fully covered within a single financial year.

Revenue/operating costs result from day-to-day running of an organization, ranging from the costs of employing people through to paper clips. They normally include 'consumables'. These are the items that wear out relatively rapidly or are low cost so that depreciation is not worth tracking, i.e. those items that are effectively fully depreciated within a single financial year.

National government fiscal policies or a service provider's own organization-wide policies normally determine the rules on revenue versus capital. The rules mean that a service provider always classes an item in the same way, irrespective of who purchases it and how it is used. The rules include a minimum cost below which an item is automatically classed as a revenue cost, even if it is an item that otherwise fits the definition of a financial asset and therefore a capital cost. This makes the accounting process simpler and therefore cheaper, because financial assets with trivial value do not have to be depreciated. Rules also define the term over which financial assets are depreciated, e.g. is a PC depreciated over 3 or 5 years.

[1] Note the life of an asset on the books can differ from the physical state of the asset.

Fixed and variable costs

There are two other categories of costs: fixed and variable. These are separated out as the accounting process manages these costs differently. Each organization may have different rules on the differences between fixed and variable costs, and therefore how costs are classified. Typical examples are described below.

Fixed cost

These are costs that can change within a budget period but do no not vary with usage or throughput of work. Examples include basic staff salaries and office rent. A basic staff salary may change if a person is promoted, but is fixed however many hours the person works. Similarly, office rent may increase but will not normally be affected if the number of people using the accommodation changes during the financial year.

Variable cost

These are costs incurred each time a service is used or a product produced. They often change within budget periods, although efforts are made to accurately predict the likely costs for each of these and the use of them may be controlled during a budget year if the actual costs vary compared to the budgeted costs. Examples include staff overtime, stationery and telephone bills. Staff overtime is often predicted as part of the budgeting process and may change according to the season, major changes to the service or an operational crisis. The variable nature of staff overtime is in contrast to the fixed costs of basic staff salaries. Similarly, while office rent will remain fixed even if more people use the office, stationery costs and telephone bills will vary.

Direct and indirect costs

Two other classifications used are direct and indirect costs. These are used to separate out how costs are attributed within an organization and are referred to in ISO/IEC 20000-1.

Direct cost

These are attributable in full to a single product, service, customer, cost centre or activity, e.g. a group of staff dedicated to developing a service to be used by a single customer group. A direct cost is more easily handled within the financial process, as there is no ambiguity about what created and influenced that cost.

Indirect cost

This term is used to describe any costs incurred on behalf of a number of products, services, customers, cost centres or business activities. The costs are shared (apportioned) among them. For example, the cost of a service desk used by several customers is commonly an indirect cost. These costs are inherently more complex to handle within financial processes as the sharing (apportioning), requires rules to be developed which may be the subject of considerable discussion before and possibly even after agreement is reached.

Balance sheet

A balance sheet is a snapshot of a service provider's financial status at a specific moment in time, usually at the close of an accounting period. A balance sheet comprises assets owned by the organization, liabilities, and owners' or stockholders' equity. (Liabilities are the claims of creditors against the assets of the service provider.) A balance sheet shows the financial strength and capabilities of the service provider's organization.

Profit and loss accounts are part of the balance sheet and report on the service provider's profit on sales and the costs of their service normally during a single financial year.

Small service providers with simple financial records may find it convenient to use a balance sheet as part of audit evidence, although there are no ISO/IEC 20000 requirements or recommendations that refer directly to a balance sheet.

CHAPTER 3

Policy, process and procedures

Introduction

This chapter describes the role and importance of financial policies in directing the underpinning processes and procedures covered by ISO/IEC 20000. Example policies are described as illustrations of the management direction required by ISO/IEC 20000.

Why policy, process and procedure?

Policy, process and procedure are important to the whole of service management, including financial processes.

ISO/IEC 20000 uses the terms 'policy', 'process' and 'procedure' in the way they are used in other management system standards. It is important to be clear on the differences between the three to understand the role each plays in requirements and in managing the end-to-end service.

Definition: Policy, process and procedure

- '**Policy**' describes the overall intentions and direction of a service provider and is formally expressed by senior management. Policies should be underpinned by processes.
- '**Process**' describes an activity using resources to transform inputs to outputs. Often, the output from one process will directly form the input into the next process. Where this is the case, the processes are integrated, can be managed properly and will be more effective overall.
- '**Procedure**' describes the specified way of carrying out a process; a procedure underpins a process.

The link between policy, process and procedure is important for all service management processes as it provides a regulatory framework for the organization's obligations for financial probity, and also for best practice service management. The relationship is shown in Figure 1.

Policies must be underpinned by processes so that management direction cascades through the service provider's day-to-day activities. The output from one process (typically information in reports) may be input to another process. Where this is the case the processes are integrated, will be more effective overall and can be managed end-to-end. The ISO/IEC 20000 auditor will assess how well underpinning processes and procedures support policies. An auditor would also expect to assess the processes by checking the actual practices against the documentation.

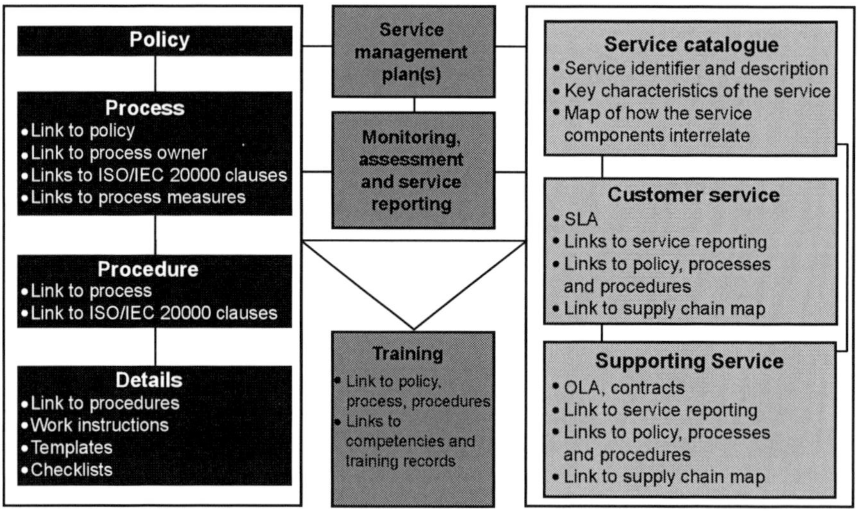

Figure 1 – Relationship between policy, process and procedure

Organization-wide policies

Financial policies may not actually be titled 'policy', particularly if they are organization-wide policies. For example, they may be termed 'Corporate policies' or be part of a single composite policy and procedure document referred to as 'Financial procedures'. As long as they serve the purpose of describing the overall intentions and direction of management they are suitable as evidence of financial policies for an ISO/IEC 20000 audit.

It is common for financial policies to be set for the whole of an organization, i.e. a wider scope than the departments who are responsible for service management. This is because the organization-wide policies are driven by the business need for regulatory and legal compliance. Organization-wide policies are therefore usually outside the direct control of those managers responsible for service management processes, but they are as relevant to requirements as policies developed within service management, for service management.

Although ISO/IEC 20000 requires policies to be established, understood and supported by processes and procedures, it does not require financial policies to be directly controlled by managers responsible for service management. Examples of financial policies that affect service management but which usually lie outside service management include:

- the rules on what is to be classed as revenue and what is classed as capital;
- depreciation terms for financial assets;
- whether services should be charged for and, if they are chargeable, the charging policies to be adopted.

Gaps in organization-wide policies

Organization-wide policies on financial management may not cover all topics specified by ISO/IEC 20000, if policies have been developed with other needs in mind. Where an organization-wide policy does not meet the needs of a service provider aiming for ISO/IEC 20000, the manager(s) responsible for service management must develop local, specific service management policies that fill the gap.

Supplementing organization-wide policies with locally established service management policies meets the requirements of ISO/IEC 20000 as long as the local service management policies are aligned and do not conflict with the corporate policies.

e.g.

Example: Organization-wide policies and service management

If a new organization-wide financial policy is introduced it could affect the provision of facilities, functions such as human resources and the delivery of technology and technology-based services. For example, if a new policy included a management directive on tracking the costs of all services, such as:

'… all costs must be tracked at departmental level in order to also understand costs at departmental level …'

the budgeting and accounting processes must change to support the new policy, as would other service management processes. For example, in order to track costs for each department using a support service the details logged by the service desk will need to be linked to the department of the user requesting support. To do this requires an accurate link between a user's name and their department, even if this information is not required for incident management.

Other service management processes, such as configuration and change management, need to ensure that the link between a user and their department was kept up to date.

The service reporting process needs to produce a report showing service usage and costs by department.

If any of these underpinning processes and procedures did not support the new financial policy, the cost data provided would be suspect, and the policy would not be implemented properly and therefore requirements specified by ISO/IEC 20000-1 would not be met.

Successful implementation of an organization-wide policy of this type normally requires significant effort on the part of the service provider. However, the service provider will receive better cost information as differences between departments will be understood, and the information can also be useful for identifying ways of reducing costs.

Key point:

An organization-wide policy on all costs being available at departmental level also means that costs, such as accommodation, become available to the service provider for calculations of the true (or total) cost of each service. This information could also be used for notional or real charging should this be considered appropriate.

Accountancy practices

ISO/IEC 20000-1 includes a note[2] that states a service provider should align all their service management accounting practices to the wider accounting practices of their whole organization.

As an organization's accounting practices are normally determined by the need to meet regulatory and legal requirements defined by professional accountancy bodies[3] for regulatory or legal requirements, there are few circumstances when this approach would not be appropriate.

The alignment with wider accounting practices in turn shapes the budgeting and accounting procedures within the scope of an ISO/IEC 20000 audit, with alignment usually being a business requirement of the service provider.

Policies required by ISO/IEC 20000-1

Budgeting and accounting policies

ISO/IEC 20000-1 includes requirements for policies and procedures to be in place for budgeting and accounting for all components of the service. Typical examples of items that fall into each type referred to by ISO/IEC 20000 are given in Chapter 4.

Policies on apportioning and allocating costs

ISO/IEC 20000-1 requires the service provider to have a policy on apportioning and allocating costs, as explained in Chapter 4. This is important even if a service provider uses only notional charging or does not charge at all, as apportioning and allocating costs is a part of understanding the reasons for costs and therefore helps identify how costs can be reduced or avoided.

[2] ISO/IEC 20000-1 is a specification of requirements that need to be met. These are all worded as 'shall'. Notes in Part 1 are, either supporting explanations or recommendations for how requirements may be met. Notes do not change the requirements and can be ignored. More information on the language used in standards is given in BIP 0030, *Management decisions and documentation.*

[3] In the UK this includes bodies such as the Financial Reporting Council, and CIPFA in the public sector. Other bodies are involved outside the UK.

Financial control and authorization policies

ISO/IEC 20000-1 requires policies and processes for effective financial control and authorization, as described in Chapter 6. This is not only because financial controls play a part in preventing fraud, but also that controls are important to service management because they provide an audit trail on who made what decision, when they made it and normally, why.

Policies recommended by ISO/IEC 20000-2

In addition to the policies that are required by ISO/IEC 20000-1, ISO/IEC 20000-2 recommends that the service provider also puts in place some additional policies, as described below.

Objectives of budgeting and accounting

ISO/IEC 20000-2 recommends that financial policies define the objectives to be met by budgeting and accounting as described in Chapter 5.

Level of detail for budgeting and accounting data

ISO/IEC 20000-2 recommends that there should be a policy on the level and type of detail used for budgeting and accounting, taking into consideration granularity of the customer's business against which costs are attributed and apportioned, as described in Chapter 4. For example, a customer business unit as one unit, subdivided into department, or by locations. This is recommended because too little or too much detail (or the wrong detail) can be a serious barrier to effective service management.

Handling variances

It is also recommended by ISO/IEC 20000-2 that financial control and authorization includes rules governing the handling of variances against budgets, e.g. the size of variance that will be escalated to senior management, as described in Chapter 4 and Chapter 5.

CHAPTER 4

Planning for effective financial control

Introduction

This chapter describes the approach to planning for financial control and decision making in service management, the reasons for the ISO/IEC 20000 requirements and recommendations, cost models and the level of decisions on the level of detail required for service management information.

Regardless of whether a service provider uses notional charging, real charging or does not charge at all, each service needs funding and requires a budget.

Designing a budget requires clarity on the cost types and level of detail that will be required for financial processes, for reporting and by other service management processes and the PDCA cycle. Decisions on cost types and on service reporting are closely linked, and one should not be agreed without reference to the other.

Budgeting and accounting processes benefit from the development of a cost model that can be used to calculate the cost of service provision, as described in later in this chapter in *Apportioning and allocating costs*. Good financial data from budgeting and accounting means management decision making will be better, including decisions on day-to-day running of the services or investments.

Budgetary figures may also provide a basis for delegating control in financial processes. For example, the level of seniority to agree a budget, the roles and responsibilities, and who is accountable when a variance occurs between actual costs and budgeted costs, as described in this chapter. Methods of mapping out service management roles and responsibilities are described in BIP 0031, *Why people matter*.

Cost models and cost types

In order to understand and manage service costs, it is necessary to agree the components of the total cost, based on components of the service. To gain the benefits of this understanding it is necessary to not only decide what cost types are required, but also how each type is costed. This is what is commonly referred to as a cost model.

The cost model should reflect the way costs behave in the real world. If this is not so a service provider or customer might be faced with unexpected costs. For example, if the service provider has not correctly identified which costs are fixed or variable and which are direct or indirect, then they might not understand the cost implications of decommissioning an application for both themselves and their customers.

In addition, an understanding of how money flows through the service provider's organization can also provide an insight into the supply chain, especially by identifying major cost drivers that can lead to major increases in value for money.

Cost types

ISO/IEC 20000 requires costs to be budgeted for in sufficient detail to enable effective financial control and decision making, with clear policies and processes for budgeting and accounting for all components. To do this, costs are categorized using consistent and easily understandable cost types. Budgeting is then done at cost type level.

Although there is no single generic set of cost types that work for every service provider, ISO/IEC 20000-1 refers to seven common cost types: IT assets, shared resources, overheads, externally supplied services, people, insurance, licences. These types are described below.

IT assets

The term 'assets' is defined in Chapter 2. For an audit, the assets that fall into this category are assets used in the delivery of the service, such as servers, printers, PCs and communications devices. Assets owned by a customer or a third-party supplier rather than the service provider may be managed by the service provider's service management and financial processes, but are not included in the service provider's financial records or budget as an asset. These assets may still have an impact on service management. For example, configuration management may track and manage assets such as printers bought directly by the customer without the involvement of the service provider who supports them.

Shared resources
Most services use resources shared by many users and some use resources used by several different customer groups. Examples include application servers, mainframes, service desks, WANs.

Overheads
Overheads are sometimes referred to as indirect costs. Overheads are the service provider's expenses and costs that are not directly associated with services but which are costs of providing a service, such as office accommodation. By their nature, they are costs that cannot be attributed directly to a service or a particular customer or department. Some overheads are capital assets owned by the service provider, e.g. a social centre owned by the service provider and used by the service provider's staff. This is an asset that will be depreciated but is also classified as an overhead for the budgeting and accounting processes. Assets of this type increase the service provider's total costs and should be taken into account when monitoring the true (or total) cost of ownership and cannot be ignored by a service provider just because it is completely non-technical and only indirectly linked to the cost of a service.

Externally supplied services
Services from an external supplier are a cost to the service provider as they represent part of the overall cost of the service. They are kept as a separate cost type because each supplier is external to the service provider's organization and each has a separate contract (which covers the charges made by the supplier) which has to be managed by the supplier management process. The role of third-party suppliers is described in BIP 0033, *Managing end-to-end service.* The service from a supplier can be fixed price/flat rate, time and materials, based on the volume of activity, open book/fixed margin or a combination of methods. An appropriate mechanism has to be used to fund and account for these costs, and if it is the service provider's policy to do so, to pass the costs onto customers.

People
The people who provide the service have a range of associated costs – basic employment costs, overtime, with special allowances and contribution to pensions being the most common features. People costs are normally a substantial proportion of a service provider's total costs.

Insurance

A policy on insurance may be as simple as 'we do not insure items below a set value', or may be a complex set of management requirements. Some service providers treat insurance as an overhead. If a service provider aiming to achieve ISO/IEC 20000 has an organization-wide policy that classifies insurance in this way, they are advised to make sure the auditor has access to mapping of the cost types references in ISO/IEC 20000 and the types used under the direction of the organization-wide policies.

If the service provider's policies require insurance, the policy must be supported by a process and the insurance premiums and any claims must be handled through service management processes. If the service provider opts not to insure, this must also be defined in a financial policy.

Self-insurance is an option that is also valid for achieving ISO/IEC 20000, i.e. opting for holding funds to cover the costs of repairs or replacements of items that could be insured under a policy with a separate organization, or not insured at all if the service provider considers the risk is low.

Licences

Licences can be a substantial proportion of the costs of delivering a service. Information on licences is required for best practice service management (i.e. are software assets being used effectively?), but this information is also required for regulatory and legal reasons.

Selecting the right cost types

For some service providers, there may need to be additional cost types. For example, a service provider may also need to include a cost type for legal costs, premises or the service provider's contribution to business continuity.

Whatever cost types are used, the full range must cover all costs and do so without ambiguity. For example, it must be clear whether or not an item falls into one cost type category or into another. This is more likely to be the case when care is taken to avoid overlapping types or types that are difficult to define.

Established cost types should only be changed when absolutely necessary, as changes to types can make it difficult to do comparisons year on year. Trend analysis may only be possible if data is manipulated to reallocate historic costs to new cost types.

Mapping cost types to ISO/IEC 20000

The seven cost types described above are typical examples and are not definitive. The service provider aiming for ISO/IEC 20000 does not need to get organization-wide policies on cost types changed in order to achieve ISO/IEC 20000. The service provider may use the cost types defined in the organization's policies. For example, a corporate policy may not recognize shared resources as a cost type and instead choose to treat all shared resources as overheads. Where this occurs it will be helpful to the auditor if there is a mapping of how their cost types map onto those listed in ISO/IEC 20000.

Cost types and the level of detail tracked for service management should be suitable for mapping costs against the services defined in service catalogues and SLAs. For example, if financial information is held and tracked at the level of types of technology, it then becomes difficult to calculate or track costs for services. Some service providers have budgets based on cost types that bear little resemblance to how they actually charge, so large approximations have to be made in calculating charges, which can in itself create dissatisfaction about the fairness of the charges.

Detailing the costs

Cost elements

In practice, cost types such as those referred to in ISO/IEC 20000 are normally broken down to lower levels of detail for the budget, as seven cost types do not give the level of detail required for the accounting process or for input to other service management processes. This lower level of detail is usually referred to as 'cost elements'. For example, cost types such as people will be subdivided into cost elements such as payroll, staff benefits, expenses, overtime and consultancy, as illustrated in Figure 2.

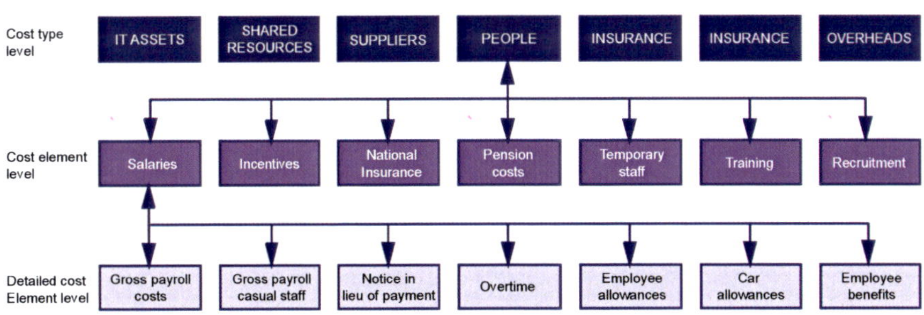

Figure 2 – Hierarchical relationship between cost types and elements

e.g.

Example: Insurance and self-insurance

An organization had insurance that covered theft and loss of technology as well as the cost of some repairs. This included a minimum amount of €700 per claim. Once notebooks and PDAs were in common use, the number of claims for lost devices rose sharply. When the insurance premium was due for renewal the insurance company increased the minimum for each device to €2,000. This meant most losses were lower than the minimum to be paid and in effect a claim could not be made for most lost or stolen devices.

The service provider did some financial modelling of the likely costs and benefits of continuing to insure such items. It was concluded that they would be financially better off to exclude notebooks and PDAs from the insurance policy, and the insurance premium would be smaller with a projected saving larger than the total claims that would be allowed with the new minimum of €2,000 per device.

Under the new policy and process, the funds that would have been budgeted for insurance for all notebooks and PDAs were spread across each department, with each department's share being based on the number of devices in use within it.

Instead of making insurance claims for loss or theft, each department was required to adopt a new procedure in which they each funded replacement notebooks and PDAs, with authorization for replacements restricted to each head of department. A publicity campaign within the organization gave two months notice of the change to policy.

As this new policy and process was implemented, the cost of notebooks and PDAs started to decrease, making new and replacement items cheaper. Repairs for the devices were funded out of the day-to-day operational support budget.

Key point:

The organization found that not only did they make small savings on the cost of the insurance premium, but that the embarrassment of having to admit that an asset such as a notebook (potentially holding confidential company data) had been lost was so great that most users started to take much greater care of their notebooks and PDAs. The rate at which items were reported as lost or stolen dropped to less than 50% of the previous year. This financial benefit was much greater than the savings for giving up the insurance, and also had the benefit of reducing the risk of loss of confidential company data on lost or stolen devices.

A small set of cost types and cost elements are illustrated in Figures 3 and 4. The figures show how the data at each level has a hierarchical relationship to other levels. From a top-down perspective, each level is split into more detail in the level below. Processes, including financial reporting, may then aggregate data according to the information required, guided by the logic of the hierarchical relationship.

Tracking financial data at a more detailed level means that it can be used more flexibly, so that data can be aggregated according to different needs, e.g. the same data analysed in one way can give a view of the costs per item of technology, re-analysed it can give the cost per customer group.

In Figure 3, the relationship between higher and lower levels, typical of a basic budget, illustrates some of the elements that, when aggregated, form the higher cost types.

In this case, the data has been analysed so that it could provide information on the proportion of costs incurred by each cost type.

In Figure 4, the relationship between higher and lower levels allows re-analysis so that data is presented with a different view so the information can be used for other purposes. In this case, the data has been re-analysed so that it could provide a basis for charging.

Actuals (Jan–Jun) / Budget forecast (Jul–Dec)

Cost type	Jan	Feb	Mar	Apr	May	Jun	Jul	Aug	Sep	Oct	Nov	Dec	Total
IT ASSETS	121,705	118,587	117,198	118,735	112,755	120,278	104,091	102,847	99,709	99,709	99,394	99,394	1,314,401
SHARED RESOURCES	103,872	101,210	100,026	101,337	96,233	102,654	88,839	87,777	85,098	85,098	84,830	84,830	1,121,805
3rd PARTY SUPPLIERS	191,763	186,850	184,663	187,084	177,661	189,515	164,010	162,050	157,105	157,105	156,610	156,610	2,071,024
PEOPLE	747,877	728,715	720,185	729,626	692,880	739,107	639,638	631,994	612,709	612,709	610,777	610,777	8,076,994
INSURANCE	13,355	13,013	12,860	13,029	12,373	13,198	11,422	11,286	10,941	10,941	10,907	10,907	144,232
LICENCES	60,803	59,245	58,552	59,319	56,332	60,090	52,003	51,382	49,814	49,814	49,657	49,657	656,666
OVERHEADS	39,570	38,556	38,105	38,605	36,660	39,106	33,843	33,439	32,418	32,418	32,316	32,316	427,354

Actuals (Jan–Jun) / Budget forecast (Jul–Dec)

People cost elements	Jan	Feb	Mar	Apr	May	Jun	Jul	Aug	Sep	Oct	Nov	Dec	Total
SALARIES	551,860	533,546	528,487	560,322	531,057	534,524	465,847	465,847	465,847	465,847	465,847	465,847	6,034,877
INCENTIVES	48,437	46,608	21,647	53,365	39,115	29,315	2,500	2,500	2,500	2,500	2,500	2,500	253,488
NATIONAL INSURANCE	55,207	54,694	44,801	62,955	47,349	56,605	56,605	53,962	53,468	53,468	51,537	51,537	642,188
PENSION COSTS	1,430	1,569	1,631	1,213	1,421	1,397	1,420	1,420	1,420	1,420	1,420	1,420	17,181
TEMPORARY STAFF	54,620	54,755	85,165	9,186	32,613	60,805	56,805	51,805	33,014	33,014	33,014	33,014	537,809
TRAINING	30,724	29,543	31,694	32,336	33,825	24,215	24,215	24,215	24,215	24,215	24,215	24,215	327,626
RECRUITMENT	5,600	8,000	6,760	10,250	7,500	32,245	32,245	32,245	32,245	32,245	32,245	32,245	263,825

Actuals (Jan–Jun) / Budget forecast (Jul–Dec)

Salaries detailed cost elements	Jan	Feb	Mar	Apr	May	Jun	Jul	Aug	Sep	Oct	Nov	Dec	Total
GROSS PAYROLL COSTS	458,814	445,915	446,822	445,454	443,015	442,746	411,216	411,216	411,216	411,216	411,216	411,216	5,150,060
GROSS PAYROLL - CASUAL STAFF	15,213	15,213	15,213	49,456	49,456	49,456	26,054	26,054	26,054	26,054	26,054	26,054	350,329
NOTICE IN LIEU OF PAYMENT	0	0	0	0	6,053	0	0	0	0	0	0	0	6,053
OVERTIME	68,538	63,846	58,311	56,504	17,790	22,929	20,126	20,126	20,126	20,126	20,126	20,126	408,674
EMPLOYEE ALLOWANCES	1,879	1,059	702	603	8,710	13,632	2,500	2,500	2,500	2,500	2,500	2,500	41,584
CAR ALLOWANCES	6,016	6,266	6,266	7,260	5,102	4,944	4,711	4,711	4,711	4,711	4,711	4,711	64,117
EMPLOYEE BENEFITS	1,400	1,248	1,172	1,045	931	817	1,241	1,241	1,241	1,241	1,241	1,241	14,060

Figure 3 – Cost types and elements in a budget

Cost types

Dept./Cost code name	Cost code	% of PCs supported	IT ASSETS	SHARED RESOURCES	3rd PARTY SUPPLIERS	PEOPLE	INSURANCE	LICENCES	OVERHEADS	TOTAL CHARGE
Facilities	1012	4.9	64,406	54,968	101,480	395,773	7,067	32,177	20,940	676,811
Field staff	1013	4.9	64,406	54,968	101,480	395,773	7,067	32,177	20,940	676,811
Head office	1014	15.8	207,675	177,245	327,222	1,276,165	22,789	103,753	67,522	2,182,371
HR	1015	3.9	51,262	43,750	80,770	315,003	5,625	25,610	16,667	538,687
Research	1016	5.9	77,550	66,186	122,190	476,543	8,510	38,743	25,214	814,936
Retail	1017	32.1	421,923	360,099	664,799	2,592,715	46,298	210,790	137,181	4,433,805
Sales	1018	12.1	159,043	135,738	250,594	977,316	17,452	79,457	51,710	1,671,310
Security	1019	1.9	24,974	21,314	39,349	153,463	2,740	12,477	8,120	262,437
Strategy	1020	3.5	46,004	39,263	72,486	282,695	5,048	22,983	14,957	483,437
Supply	1021	15	197,160	168,271	310,654	1,211,549	21,635	98,500	64,103	2,071,871
Total			1,314,401	1,121,805	2,071,024	8,076,994	144,232	656,666	427,354	13,812,476

Dept./cost codes

Figure 4 – Re-analysis of cost elements in a budget

Judging the right detail

Policies on the level and nature of detail will vary from one service provider to another as each service provider faces different requirements and has different financial information needs. Very little data may be required when simple identification of costs is sufficient. Conversely, too little detail may mean the financial information is inadequate for use by the other service management processes.

Collecting and analysing data to an unnecessary level of detail adds costs without adding benefits to the service and may degrade the efficiency of processes. Conversely, having too little information on costs and budget status means decisions are made with incomplete information, value for money cannot be reliably assessed and changes may degrade efficiency, rather than improving it.

The service provider's process owners need an understanding of the strengths and weakness of any resource and cost monitoring tools so that the level of detail required for implementation of financial policies is based on a realistic understanding of the costs and benefits of collecting financial data for use in service management. An auditor would expect to see evidence that the level of detail is appropriate to meet the financial policies and for use of the information service level management and business relationship management.

The level of detail also needs to be understood when decisions are being made on investment in budgeting and accounting processes, e.g. the number of people that will be required for carrying out each aspect of the financial process and for purchase and continuing support of financial management tools. It is also important to include the costs of changes to other service management processes that rise as a result of changes to financial policies, processes or tools, e.g. the need to track more details for each incident and service request in order to track costs.

Customer and supplier interests

ISO/IEC 20000-2 recommends that financial policies on the level and type of detail to be budgeted and accounted for are also based on an understanding of the financial detail required by the customer and supplier, not just on the service provider's own needs. This may also mean that data has to be tracked and held at lower cost element levels.

e.g. Example: Judging the right amount of detail

A service provider had received many complaints from their customer's most senior management that the service was too expensive. Costs were covered as overheads in the customer's budget. Management saw the overheads in the budget and accounts but users had no knowledge at all of costs.

Service management had been partially implemented, with basic service level agreements (SLAs) agreed, but not connected in any way to costs.

In order to identify how the service could be made cost effective, senior management appointed a process owner tasked with improving the financial information available. This work was sponsored by the most senior manager in the service provider's organization.

The original view was that costs would have to be tracked at very low levels of detail in order to pinpoint exactly how, where and by who costs were incurred. For specialist software, this was relatively easy and specialist software teams were easily identified and an approximation could be made on their additional costs, such as office accommodation. However, the process owner realized there was a greater challenge in how detailed information could be obtained for standard services such as use of PCs and email. To accurately link the actual cost of supporting each user to an individual was rapidly seen to be impractical.

Instead the process owner was able to track the number of PCs and email IDs used by each department, developing a simple cost model that allowed apportionment of costs to each department. It was accepted that some departments were more expensive to support than others, but to achieve greater accuracy would increase the cost of tracking the information by an order of at least 10. The process owner got the support of the senior manager who sponsored the work. The senior manager then ensured there was agreement on the new cost model and how it would be used as part of planning to improve the service. After some additional refinement, the cost model was linked to the SLAs and used in notional charging.

Key point:

The balance between the cost of tracking the details and the benefit sought from this was carefully judged with any potential errors understood and managed. This approach of identifying and agreeing the optimum detail provided many benefits to service management and allowed the service provider to identify cost savings with the minimum increase in the cost of the financial process.

Charging and level of detail

Where the service provider does either notional charging or real charging, the basis of charging needs to be linked to the cost data that is tracked and reported. Unless there is a link, the level and type of cost data may be unsuitable for the charging mechanism used. When charges are based on incorrect or inappropriate cost data there could be challenges to the price charged from the customers. This may also extend to challenges on the actual basis and principles of charging.

For example, is the customer's organization several different business units, each with very different services, so that each should be tracked separately? Is each business unit further divided into different functional units with localized cost control and cost centres, so greater granularity is required for cost tracking? Should charging be influenced by location?

Commercial service providers may also need to invest more time and effort and to have some automation in place so that they can justify the charges and link them to the terms of their contract.

Apportioning and allocating costs

When developing a cost model it is important to understand how overheads/indirect costs are apportioned. This may affect the cost model. These are costs that cannot be directly linked to a single service, or customer, but which are incurred as part of normal operations and are incurred on behalf of a number of products, services, customers and cost centres or business activities.

Apportioning indirect costs means the costs are shared according to established rules, normally agreed when the new costs are first included in a budget. The method of apportioning indirect costs should be representative of how costs are incurred in the real world. If this is not so, changes in activity might result in unexpected changes in costs.

Even if the service provider does not charge, or only uses notional charging, apportionment and allocation of costs must still be done correctly, so that the process is fair and unambiguous. This provides better information for setting new budgets or making investment decisions.

Typical methods of apportioning costs include flat rate, fixed percentage, or costs based on the size of a variable element such as the number of people using the service.

The decision on how to apportion costs is normally based on the best balance between:

- accuracy of tracking;
- cost of tracking;
- benefits gained from understanding costs and how they are incurred.

e.g. Example: A new cost model and apportionment of overheads

A service provider had calculated the cost of a help desk using a very simple but effective cost model used for service management planning, in which costs such as the help desk were classified by:

- people, split into basic salary with employment overheads, overtime and 'other costs';
- support technology;
- accommodation, split into a nominal office rent and the cost of fixtures and fittings.

As a result of a major service improvement programme, the service provider changed the original help desk from a simple log and refer function to a service desk that resolved over 75% of the incidents, problems and service requests remotely, including a very high first-time fix rate.

This part of the service improvement programme altered the proportion of staff on the front line compared to second and third level support teams, so that the service desk became a much higher proportion of the total costs compared to the help desk it replaced. Although this was considered to represent improved value for money, the service provider was unable either to understand underlying cost drivers or to justify claims that it represented value for money. The change programme had required a major programme of investment in remote support technology and management time on the organizational changes. There were also new costs from an incentive scheme introduced to encourage the service desk staff to achieve a high remote fix rate.

The service provider redesigned their cost model, introducing more detailed cost types and elements for the costs of the service desk, second and third line support teams. The costs of new remote support technology were also assessed, and new rules were developed for how costs such as the new remote support technology were apportioned across each support team.

The service provider was able to develop a cost model that was sufficiently flexible for costs to be understood for each support team, for each of the major services and for each department in the customer's business. This level of flexibility in how financial information could be assessed, allowed service improvements to be based on better workload management, avoidance of incidents and faster problem management. It also allowed the service provider to calculate the true cost of ownership of key items of technology and important key performance indicators such as the unit costs of resolution of incidents and cost norms for implementing commonly requested changes. Basic but effective information was made available to the service level management and business relationship management processes.

Key point:

The service provider realized the importance of having cost information and a flexible cost model as part of their overall service management, and in particular as part of their service improvement programmes. They were able to project and then prove the cost-benefit and value for money of additional service improvements, including those that required the involvement and cooperation of the customers and users.

ISO/IEC 20000 does not specify under what rules apportionment and allocation should be done, only that the service provider is required to have a policy that reflects the need for information on costs, as described in Chapter 3. Each service provider must therefore make a judgment on this based on their circumstances.

Service providers that use too simplistic a basis for apportioning and allocating costs may find the business relationship management process will be taken up by dealing with complaints that the costs are not fair. Conversely, those that use a complex basis may find the costs of doing so outweigh any benefits from having access to detailed financial information. This is particularly the case for apportionment of indirect costs as generally allocation of direct costs is less contentious, even if unwelcome. Even where a customer is not actually being charged for a service, arguments can arise over the handling of overhead costs.

An auditor will seek evidence that the apportionment of indirect costs and allocation of direct costs is done according to the service provider's normal practices (normally defined in a policy) and that the method of apportioning and allocation is understood when cost data is used in the PDCA cycle.

Using a cost model

Cost models are most useful when they are flexible enough for analysis to be able to show costs grouped in more than one way, e.g. the cost of each service, the cost for each customer, the cost for each type of technology or the cost for each location. The cost model is also most useful if it can be used to predict the costs of changed services, especially as costed options. Figure 5 illustrates the relationship between various cost types, cost elements, direct and indirect costs.

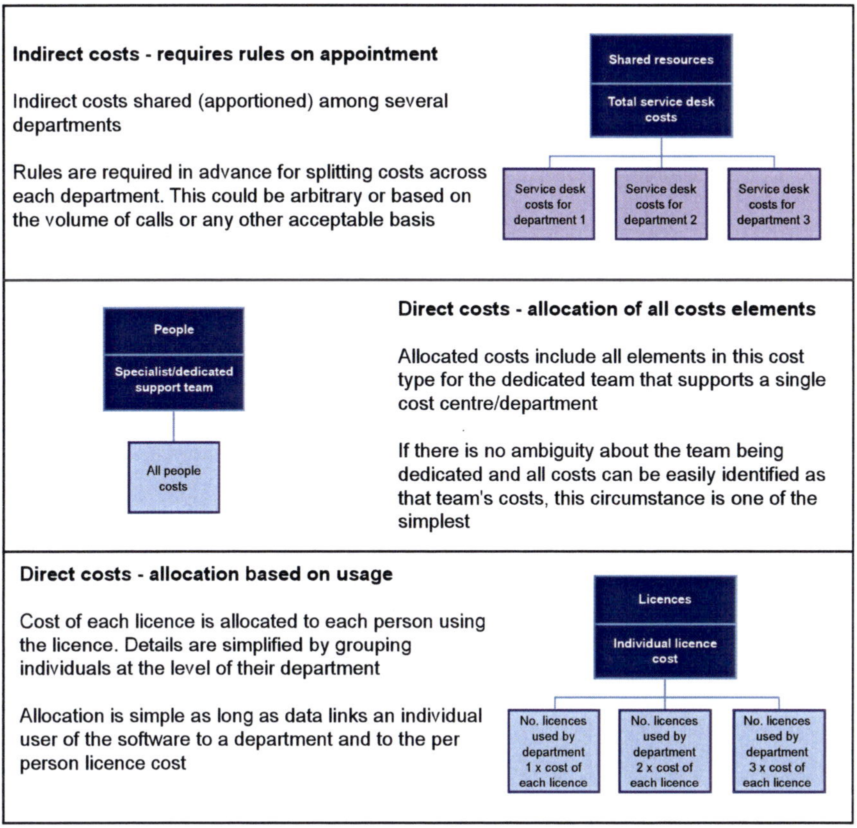

Figure 5 – Cost model relationship

The cost model should also reflect the way costs impact the choices people make as a result of the costs being incurred, even if those costs are not treated as charges. If this is not the case, a service provider may be faced with unexpected costs that are widely different from those forecast and included in the budget. For example, if the service provider has not correctly identified which costs are fixed or variable, and which are direct or indirect, then the cost implications of changes during the budget year may not be understood – such as decommissioning an application.

CHAPTER 5

Budgeting and accounting processes

Introduction

Possessing good financial data means decisions on services or investments can be made on a reliable basis. For example, the cost of a new service in the coming financial year, a project to deliver service improvements or a project required for a service provider to achieve ISO/IEC 20000.

This chapter describes the ISO/IEC 20000 requirements for establishing a budget and the accounting process, and the reasons for these requirements.

Establishing a budget

What makes a good budget?

Budgeting for service management is intended to ensure that sufficient funds are made available to provide services throughout each financial year.

If there has been good planning of cost types, elements and of rules for apportioning overheads, either within service management or as part of the organization-wide controls, a sound budget can be established. When the accounting process uses the information in the budget a good understanding of the service provider's income and costs will be available. Information from previous years can also help the financial process interpret this year's data. For example, is a change in the run rate of costs due to a seasonal change or due to an underlying change in the cost of delivering the service?

By predicting expected costs in advance of each financial year, a service provider can build a revenue/operating budget and a capital budget for the next year. Understanding the revenue/operating budget also means it is possible to build a more effective capital budget, as the nature and scale of capital investments required is influenced by an understanding of the level and type of revenue/operating costs.

The budget will hold details on the predicted (budgeted for) costs, month by month and for the whole year. Year-to-date figures are also normally included. Where depreciation is applied to capital assets, this is also shown in the capital budget.

Support for the budget

It is advisable for explanatory notes supporting the financial policy and budgeting process to make clear:

- the rules used for classifying costs as capital or revenue;
- how depreciation is calculated for each capital cost type, i.e. number of years for the expected useful working life and the algorithm that is applied to calculate depreciation over each year;
- what the link is between actual costs and the cost centres or cost codes;
- how overheads are shared (among several cost centres).

It is common for costs to be budgeted for as equal monthly amounts (1/12th of the annual costs) but this uniformity is not compulsory. A budget may show different amounts for each month, e.g. a predicted increase in support costs due to well-understood seasonal variation. Where variations are expected and included, the effort of investigating individual variances is reduced, as predicted variations are built into the budget.

Relationship to service management

The annual cycle of predicting capital and revenue costs and agreeing the actual funds to be budgeted can take several months and is frequently iterative. In best practice service management, this is linked to the review of current services, service levels, workloads and customer's activities, current and predicted. This requires integrated processes, and in particular integration of the budgeting and accounting process with the business relationship, service level and supplier management processes described in BIP 0033, *Managing end-to-end service* and in BIP 0038, *Integrated service management'.*

The accuracy with which costs can be forecast will often depend on the accuracy of data provided by the customer, mainly via the service level management and business relationship management processes, and an element of risk will always exist. Not all costs are known before the budget is agreed, many have to be estimated as accurately as possible at the time the budget is agreed, taking into account past experience or on a prediction of future activity. It is important for such predictions to be realistic, with assumptions clearly documented.

Monitoring and reporting costs

The accounting process uses the budget (i.e. the predicted costs) as financial targets against which actual costs are compared. ISO/IEC 20000 requires the accounting process to cover all the budgeted components of a service under the control of service management processes.

Best practice accounting processes enable a service provider to monitor, calculate and report the costs of a service and of its components.

This information can in turn be used to predict the costs of changes to the service, e.g. in the development of cost-benefit calculations. This normally requires information such as the cost of staff time, activity recording, costs of supplier contracts, software licensing, accommodation etc. A service manager or process owner can normally get advice on the most appropriate techniques for this from their own finance departments, e.g. return on investment (ROI). Although techniques such as ROI are often used in making investment decisions, it is also important to monitor whether or not actual ROI matches expectations.

The financial goals and projected cash flow of the budget allow financial performance to be tracked during the financial year. A sound understanding of run rate costs and capital investments is really important for meeting the requirements for effective financial control and decision making, as well as the management of the costs.

Financial reports are therefore required to:

- ensure IT service levels can be maintained;
- predict and control the money required to run IT services;
- alert the service provider to under- or over-consumption of resources;
- account for the money spent on IT services;
- provide the basis for investment decisions and costed-options;
- give an understanding of the costs of not making changes;
- give an understanding of cost-effectiveness and cost comparisons;
- help managers plan with greater confidence.

Example metrics are given in Chapter 10.

Budget variance and risk management

Financial reporting will identify gaps between the budgeted and actual funds (both income and costs) and the financial management process must react according to the risk represented by this. Accounting processes will have to investigate the reasons for differences between the budget and actual spend. This is part of financial and service risk management and is closely related to the financial responsibilities described in Chapter 6.

When actual costs are higher or lower than expected during the year, the variance[5] can be investigated, understood and managed before financial issues become significant. Using a budget in this way should mean that the correct funds are available for the provision of the agreed IT services and that the budget is not over-spent or spent incorrectly. Plans should also be put in place for managing significant variances. For example, a large difference between the actual costs and budgeted costs for the people employed by the service provider needs to be understood and managed.

The actions taken will depend on the reasons for the variance. Being under-budget is not necessarily good news, even though the service provider may be apparently running at a lower than expected cost. For example, if the budgeted costs for staff are higher than the actual run rate for staff costs, this may be due to increased and unacceptable rates of staff losses. The ability of the remaining staff to deliver to the agreed service levels will be undermined by staff losses. This is likely to be compounded by the remaining staff feeling under pressure and therefore more likely to seek a new role. In this case, the action may be a recruitment drive combined with management addressing the reasons for excessive staff turnover to stem future loses.

If the staff costs are higher than budgeted plans, this may have been due to an unexpected increase in the support workload, requiring more staff. This situation normally needs more than a simplistic cap on recruitment. For example, an investigation into why the workloads have increased may identify root causes that can be resolved so that workloads return to their previous levels. If the root cause is due to an implementation project creating increased support workload, the release and change management processes can be used to get the project-related support workload back under control.

Accounting process rules should be agreed on what is considered to be acceptable and unacceptable variances and on what should be done when an unacceptable variance is observed. This normally starts with a

[5] Term used for a gap between actual and budgeted costs.

request to explain why the variance has occurred and then may extend to referral to a more senior person. The rules on handling a variance may also include agreement on methods of capping costs mid-year, such as headcount freezes, change to a bonus or changes to a service. This is also linked to the PDCA cycle described in Chapter 8.

Underlying causes

Reasons for variance might include:

- changes in the level of customer activity;
- changes in the size of the customer's business;
- changes in the number of users;
- unexpected costs such as the need to finance response to a major disaster;
- changes in technology;
- the introduction of efficiencies (or inefficiences) into processes, e.g. for service improvements or process re-engineering;
- poor identification of actual costs during the budgeting exercise;
- overly simplistic mapping of the annual budget on to monthly accounting periods, e.g. a business that is highly seasonal should not budget $^{1}/_{12}$th of expenditure to each month.

Variances may change the projected total costs as a steady trend during the budget year or may only affect a single month's figures. For example, a trend in the cost of overheads such as telephony may be due to the change from contact with the service desk being phone-based to being mainly email-based or remote entry of requests by users. This is unlikely to represent a risk to financial management of the service, but could indicate that the budgeting process was not done with adequate information about plans for the next year.

Variances that are short term may be due to unusual events, such as a major virus outbreak requiring unusually high levels of staff overtime. This represents an immediate risk to the service, but also to the financial management and the ability of the service provider to stay within budget and keep overall costs under control. Funds reallocated to pay for this circumstance may have to be withdrawn from another initiative. Risks can be managed by information on the cost of managing the virus outbreak being used by other service management processes, so that changes to how virus outbreaks are avoided may be funded quickly, using the historic costs as part of the projected cost-benefit.

The accounting process may also need to re-forecast costs if circumstances change and to consider the impact of any changes on the budget. This does not change the actual overall funds budgeted, but makes variances easier to understand and control, once identified.

Variances in income/operating budget

Although attention is usually more readily focused on variances in costs, for service providers that operate charging regimes, variances may be in the incoming operating funds as well as in funds allocated to the service provider's costs.

These variances are as important as those arising with costs. The techniques and controls for managing the variances may be very similar, but the causes of the variances may differ. For example, where operating budget is based on the assumption that the service is funded by a per-user charge or by the number of specialist systems in operation; if this changes unexpectedly, a variance will be observed.

This may have been unpredictable (e.g. a merger kept confidential until just before it was agreed) or should have been predicted but was not (e.g. a failure to understand the customer's business plans by the business relationship management process). Either circumstance indicates that the PDCA cycle may need to review not only the financial processes, but also the other service management processes.

CHAPTER 6

Financial responsibilities

Introduction

This chapter describes the requirements and recommendations for clarity on financial responsibilities, e.g. how financial control is achieved. It also describes the importance of management commitment to best practice.

Financial responsibility is closely linked to the application of financial controls described in Chapter 4. Management of variances between budgeted funds and actual funds is described in Chapter 5.

ISO/IEC 20000 and management commitment

Management commitment to best practice processes is required for a service provider to achieve ISO/IEC 20000 and assessing this forms part of an audit. Financial processes are unlikely to achieve the standards required if the service provider's management considers financial management to be 'something the accountants do'.

ISO/IEC 20000-1, 4.1 requires a member of management to be responsible for the coordination and management of all services. ISO/IEC 20000 refers to this person as 'the senior responsible owner'. This person is accountable for the service management plan and should be supported by a decision-taking group with sufficient authority to define policy and enforce its decisions. This includes ensuring budgeting and accounting is recognized as an important service management process.

In practice it is necessary for this manager to work very closely with the service management process owners.

e.g.

Example: Process ownership

An organization had traditionally funded IT services as a company overhead. Although IT services were not considered to be business critical, costs of the service as a percentage of the total organization turnover had increased year by year, without it being understood why this was happening. The user did not know how much the service cost the organization. As the cost of internal charging was considered to be an unnecessary expense, costs were tracked in only the most simple, high level of detail. For example, costs of a help desk were tracked for the whole organization combined; applications development and maintenance were not separated as budget entries.

When the organization entered a period of financial cut backs due to a recession in their industry, the in-house service provider was required to find and make significant savings. As little cost information existed, the senior management team were unable to easily identify where savings could be made. An attempt to cut costs by reducing budgets by a flat rate for each service provider department resulted in an extended period of budget discussion and negotiation. Savings were haphazard and had an unpredictable impact on the quality of the service. Business-critical software was supported by less people as the manager had reduced the support activity in order to protect the development of a replacement system close to implementation.

As complaints from the customers increased rapidly, the IT Director decided to take an active and detailed interest in establishing more efficient service delivery and processes that could track and predict costs so that any future decisions on cost-cutting could be done on the basis of likely impact on the service and on the customer's business activity. One of the key parts of this was to get a better understanding of what created the costs and why costs had been increasing gradually. A major step was to appoint a process owner with responsibility for financial processes. This process owner worked with the other process owners and set in place a series of changes that meant costs were being monitored in greater detail. A cost model was developed that meant the costs could be linked to the customer's business activities, based on customer departments. This was relatively basic as an approach, but provided information on how costs were incurred relatively quickly.

The organization still held the view that charging, even on a notional basis, was not a policy it intended to introduce. However, the financial process owner continued tracking costs, and linking costs for each type of service to the business activity (and department) that caused the cost, e.g. by requesting a change to a system or for new technology to be used within their department. The information allowed them to identify savings by putting in place a series of service improvement initiatives. These ranged from savings from incident and problem avoidance, improvements in the time taken to resolve problems, user training targeted at customer departments that made unusually frequent requests for help because they were not trained in using the technology, through to significant savings from better control of their suppliers. The following budget year the same cost base was able to deliver a more appropriate service with higher service levels, less service losses and higher customer satisfaction.

Key point:

The organization realized they had under-estimated the importance of financial information in service management and that instead of saving money by not tracking costs, they had allowed costs to get out of control. The scale of benefits from being able to consider cost and service data during reviews of their service was so great that they again increased the level of detail and types of detail tracked, feeding this into more successful service improvement programmes. They also recognized the importance of management commitment to the changes.

Who does financial management?

For some service providers, authority and responsibility for many financial decisions lies outside the part of a service provider's organization that is responsible for service management. Final accountability for financial processes may also lie outside the departments that are normally considered to be responsible for service management, in part because of the role financial processes play in meeting legal requirements and achieving regulatory compliance. This means that service providers might need to operate financial systems that are not under their direct control. It may also be necessary for service management to supplement the existing financial information used by the service provider to manage the whole organization, in order to reach best practice service management standards.

ISO/IEC 20000 only includes requirements for processes. It does not include requirements for any particular organizational forms, or for any process to be mapped to a specific department or role. This is because there are many different ways of structuring an organization, and the way that best meets the needs of one organization may be unsuitable for another. In contrast, best practice service management processes apply equally to all service providers.

When a service provider considers 'who does financial management?', a wide variety of options are available. Some organizations choose to allocate responsibility for part of financial management to people responsible for other service management processes. For example, budgeting for additional capacity is part of the financial management process, but the actual work preparing a budget entry on this may be done by those who are also responsible for capacity management. In this approach the capacity management process would produce the information on projected capacity requirements and convert it to expected costs and a timetable for when the costs would be incurred. In this approach the same people project capacity requirements and the conversion of the predicted requirements to costs.

In an alternative approach, the financial management processes are the responsibility of a central group who receive information on plans for the next financial year from the people who are responsible for the capacity management process. When this is the case, the central group responsible for financial management would then convert the information into the required budgetary details.

The same logic applies to the interface between the financial management process and all other service management processes. Either approach is acceptable for an audit, which checks that there is no ambiguity about who does what and that authority and control requirements are understood and complied with for that particular service provider, not that specific individuals have specific responsibilities.

Financial control and authorization levels

Financial controls are not only about the prevention of fraud, they also prevent errors in the financial processes which in turn reduce the risk to the rest of service management. For example, if a manager did not understand the controls and checks required before expenditure was authorized, expenditure might be agreed that had not been properly checked and which may be in excess of the funds available. This may leave another initiative which had been through the proper control process without funds.

Compulsory financial policies on the rules for financial control and authorization of expenditure, described in Chapter 3, are also linked closely to the budgeting process, as tracking against a budget with appropriate levels of detail supports control by identifying expenditure that has not been authorized correctly.

Accounting processes also play a part in delegating control. For example, the roles, responsibilities and who is accountable when a variance occurs between actual costs and budgeted costs. Methods of mapping out roles and responsibilities are described in BIP 0031, *Why people matter*.

CHAPTER 7

Charging

Introduction

In practice, many service providers will be involved in charging for services. ISO/IEC 20000-2 recommends that where service providers have a policy of charging, the mechanism for doing so is fully defined and understood by all parties. This chapter also describes how charging may impact the way the customers view the service, their choice of technology and their use of the support service. It also describes the differences that are commonly found between commercial service providers and service providers who are part of the same organization as their customers.

ISO/IEC 20000-2 recommendations

There is no such thing as a 'free service'. Services not charged for are still paid for by an organization, but the funding may be high level with all service costs being accounted for as a small number of lines in the budget. Charges may be invisible to the users. It is common for service providers 'who do not charge for services' to know what the service costs overall, but for there to be no internal transfer of service costs against the budgets of individual user departments. Typically, when service costs are only understood at a high level, with cost tracking only of the value of assets and staff costs, the financial information used by service management is of limited value.

Although charging is optional in ISO/IEC 20000, any service provider that does charge for their service is recommended[6] to have a charging policy supported by effective processes and procedures, which are documented and understood by those affected or involved. This is included in ISO/IEC 20000-1 because of the impact that charging can have on the effectiveness of service management and how the service is used.

---

[6] This is covered by a note in ISO/IEC 20000. As it is a note, it is a recommendation.

Poor quality charging processes and procedures may also impact the service provider's budgeting and accounting. When charges are raised, it is important to provide clear and unambiguous communication to the customer, well in advance of their annual budget cycle, particularly when charging is being introduced for the first time. Charging may affect the service level management process during review of the service or during discussions of changes to the service. Other processes affected may be as diverse as the management of satisfaction with the service as part of the business relationship management process through to investment in service continuity etc. An auditor may assess the impact of the charging process on the service management.

Impact of charging

Charging is not just about recovering costs or making a profit. Charging may also influence the choice of technology, the types of service and how the technology and service are used. Charging can be used to encourage use of standard technology, to request service during core hours or to accept a lower level of service for a lower price. Before introducing charging a service provider needs to be clear about why charging is being introduced, the impact that it is expected charging will have, the charging policies it intends to establish and how policies on charging affect other service management policies. It is recommended that charging processes and procedures should:

- reflect service management policies, not just financial policies;
- result in charges that are predicable and easy to manage against a budget for both the service provider and the customer;
- provide charges in a format that is easily understood, i.e. bills easy to understand and relate to use of the service;
- recover the costs of providing services as intended;
- provide influence on the use of technology and the service.

It is advisable to have a charging regime that is seen as fair, as well as understood. Customers are also more likely to value a service when they have choices on the nature of the service. Any decision on the introduction or changes to charges should involve at least the service level and business relationship management processes.

e.g. Example: Charging influencing use of service/technology

An organization had formed from the merger of several small organizations and had a lot of legacy technology. In an attempt to unify the service across the whole organization, all support for PCs was charged at the same rate. Support for technology that was difficult to support was at the same rate as new technology that could mainly be supported remotely and therefore cheaply. A campaign to get people to use the more reliable technology was not successful, as the customers had not budgeted for new technology purchases and had paid the same charge for support regardless of how much it actually cost.

The service provider continued to support the full range of technology. This created difficulties among the support staff. Many support staff did not want to work on the old technology and those that were asked to do so were likely to leave for better career prospects. This further degraded the service for old technology as the number of staff that understood it decreased, the skill level dropped so that changes were done only with difficulty and more effort than the newer technology.

The service provider investigated the costs and realized that the new technology was five times cheaper to support than old technology. Once this was established, the service provider decided to charge a rate that reflected the effort required to support it, and at the same time to subsidize the replacement of old technology. Cost modelling predicted that this would reduce the total support costs by more than the cost of the replacements, and at the same time achieve greater standardization of technology, better opportunities for volume purchases and reduce staff turnover, providing additional financial and service benefits. This programme went exceptionally well after some initial reluctance on the customer's part.

Key point:

The service provider realized that by standardizing support costs to simplify the charging had unintentionally created a barrier to change. Linking actual costs to charges was fairer and at the same time provided a real incentive to switch to the new technology. The benefit from this approach encouraged them to use other cost data more effectively, identifying additional improvements in both the service and costs.

Basis for charging

Charging regime

Policy decisions on charging are made at a strategic level. Benefits of implementation should outweigh the cost of implementation. Charging for services will only be effective if:

- customers have budgets that cover the costs, i.e. charging should not be introduced mid-budget year unless provision has been made;
- charges are in line with use of the services;
- charges are simple, fair and sensible;
- service charges by internal service providers are seen as real costs and therefore taken seriously, i.e. funds are used that could otherwise be used for something else;
- the costs incurred by the service provider is reflected in the charges, i.e. charging that has no relationship to costs will create problems as charges cannot then be used to manage the quality and type of service used and costs may increase as a direct result;
- customer and user behaviour is influenced, e.g. more effective use of available resources or use at a more appropriate time;
- charges are not for costs over which customers have no control, i.e. if the customers cannot manage their costs the charges will create complaints and such charging cannot be used as effectively in service management;
- there is effective tracking and forecasting using cost-effective methods.

Charging policies

The processes and procedures for charging should be directed by a charging policy. Decisions that have to be made by management responsible for policy agreement may include the following.

Recovery required – all or partial
A policy of partial recovery normally only applies to in-house service providers, because commercial service providers are not in a position to intentionally under-recover their costs.

In this method, a simple charging process can be adopted that will result in only some of the total costs being recovered. For example, certain types of service are charged for and some are covered out of a central overhead budget so that individual customers or users do not receive charges for all services. Partial recovery can be used to raise awareness of service costs based on those that are easily identified and levied, so that the overhead of cost recovery is minimized. Partial recovery may also be used to encourage the use of a particular type of standardized technology.

What to charge for, i.e. how to recover costs
For either partial or full recovery charging, decisions have to be made on what to charge for.

How to charge: notional charging versus actual charging
Many in-house service providers use notional charging, in which costs are identified but funds do not move to or from internal cost codes. In real charging, funds move between cost centres or actually between separate organizations, i.e. the charges are 'real money'.

Level of accuracy and detail
As described in Chapter 4, the level of detail has to be a balance between the quality and quantity of information that is required for service management (and for regulatory or legal compliance) and the cost of providing the information. Each organization has to develop a policy on this that meets their business needs.

Pricing

If the service provider's policy is to charge for services, then a pricing policy is also required. Commonly used options include:

- cost (full or marginal);
- cost-plus (standard percentage addition or plus unpredictable costs as in a new start-up);
- 'going rate' (compared with others, such as other internal departments or similar service providers);
- market price (that charged by commercial service providers);
- fixed price (negotiated with the customer for a fixed period based on a predicted consumption).

Charging is often about influencing behaviour and may or may not be based on actual usage/effort. A service provider may decide to price some services to encourage different behaviour or choice of technology, so that the price charged is not closely linked to the actual cost incurred.

e.g.

Example: Conflict from a badly implemented charging policy

An in-house service provider had been funded for many years largely as an overhead in the organization's overall budget, with most cost types budgeted for and monitored at the level of the whole organization. Based on the volume of support requests it was believed that there was a large variety in usage of the standard services, such as PC support. Charges for the support of specialist software used by individual departments were tracked at departmental level but this represented a relatively small proportion of the total cost. Attempts had been made to reduce IT services costs by encouraging user self-help training. These attempts had either little or no effect on the service workload, as the customers did not see the advantage of using their departmental budgets to fund staff training courses because 'it's easier to ask the service desk'.

As part of a wider service improvement programme, the service provider decided to introduce a full cost pricing and charging model, with charges raised directly against each department. In this model the actual costs of standard services such as PC support would be tracked and used as the basis of prices used for charging, at departmental level, for each of 15 departments. Each department would be expected to actually pay for specialist software and support based on the costs previously reported.

Although the principle of seeking improvements to cost control was supported by each of the 15 departments affected, the programme encountered some resistance. Initially this was because the proposal that charging should be introduced was made only a few weeks before the agreement of the budget for the year when charging would be introduced. None of the departmental level budgets had allowed for this charge, all funding having been at organizational level. In order to establish the principle of charging, an interim arrangement was made by which the funds allocated at a whole organization level were allocated to each department in a proportion based on the number of PCs they had in use. The funds allocated for specialist software were similarly allocated to each department, based on historic costs adjusted to take into account business and IT plans.

This raised the profile of the relationship between use of a service and the cost of a service, but also created many difficulties for those involved in the business relationship and service level management process. It was also recognized part-way through the financial year that the count of PCs recorded as being used by each department was actually widely different to the actual number in use, the main focus in PC numbers having been previously for asset management of all the organizations assets, not a record of who used which asset. Several processes had to be improved to ensure that in future the records were correct. Improvements were required to the logging process of incident management, and the change and configuration management processes. A physical inventory was completed at the same time.

Next year the service provider was able to agree forecast funds required for budgets at departmental level, but the process was still subject to complaints. Customers frequently referred back to the previous problems and used the errors in the charging process to argue they were being overcharged. Plans to extend the charging for all services to departmental level had to be stopped until the disagreements on the earlier charging had been resolved.

Key point:

The service provider realized that many of the problems they encountered were rooted in attempting to impose a charging regime at short notice and without first planning carefully what they needed to do. With hindsight they realized a simple cost model would have highlighted the need for an accurate configuration, asset data and historical information on actual costs per department, and that they should have given sufficient notice for each department to be able to budget for their new departmental costs.

Differences between commercial and in-house service providers

In-house service provider

Many in-house service providers use notional charging. This does not normally affect the amount of funds available to and controlled by each cost centre, as the charge is notional, i.e. it is not 'real money'. However, it does make all managers aware of the cost of the service. This is often used as a stage in the introduction of full charging to an organization. This is useful for any organization where the policy is not to charge for internal services so that managers and users do not see a link between their use of the service and how much it will be costing their own organization.

In these circumstances, providing this information may encourage cost saving initiatives within the customer's own business units. Examples include more careful priorities being set for technology-based investments, such as new functions in systems, printers being shared and deletion or off line archiving of files to reduce online storage space.

Other in-house service providers use internal charge transfers, in which charges are calculated then debited from the customer's cost centre and credited to the service provider's cost centre. This charge being debited reduces the funds that are under the direct control of that cost centre and although cash neither leaves nor enters the organization on the whole it is seen by the manager as 'real money'.

Cost management and reduction initiatives are more likely to be supported when the funds transferred are seen as 'real money'. Depending on the organization's policies on cost recovery, it may be possible for an in-house service provider to make a surplus on one part of the service to balance out a loss on another part.

Commercial service providers

A commercial service provider is by definition a separate legal entity to their customer(s) and so charges mean funds of some sort actually flow from the customer to the service provider as each charge is levied using some form of invoicing. This is 'real money' in every sense.

Organizations who believe they have not been able to get adequate information on costs from their service provider may change provider, selecting the new service provider because they are able to give the desired information.

Other differences exist, e.g. some service agreements link service levels or other key performance indicators to financial incentives or penalties. These can be applied where any 'real money' is transferred, either between cost centres or more commonly between a commercial service provider and their customer.

CHAPTER 8

The Plan-Do-Check-Act (PDCA) cycle

Introduction

This chapter describes the role of the PDCA cycle and its relationship to financial processes. It also describes how changes to the service, often identified under the PDCA cycle, rely on the use of financial information for fully informed decision making.

It is important that even if a service provider does not charge for services, costs should be understood. Linking cost to activity is an important part of setting priorities, helping to manage finances on an ongoing basis and deciding what options you have when trying to manage down overspend/variances.

The cost of services

If the organization does not charge for all costs, e.g. for the accommodation used by the IT department, it is advisable for IT to make a provision for such costs in its own financial system so that the true costs of the service are understood and can be used in management decisions.

Finance and the PDCA cycle

The PDCA cycle requirements of ISO/IEC 20000-1 mean that a service provider should continually improve their service, as shown in Figure 6.

Under the PDCA cycle, financial processes should also be reviewed and improved, but the implications for service management and financial processes are much wider. The PDCA cycle includes access to sound financial management and cost awareness when considering service changes and service improvements. The PDCA cycle also covers improvements in the effectiveness (and efficiency) of service management processes. This in turn relies on information on service costs to be provided by the financial processes. This financial information can be used to prove or improve value for money, either within the financial process or within one of the other service management processes.

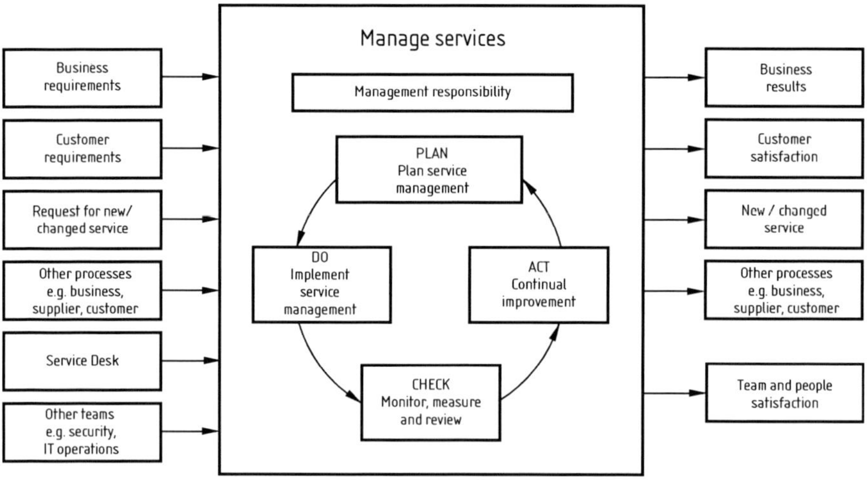

Figure 6 – The Plan-Do-Check-Act cycle

The service provider is able to develop costed-options, which can then become the basis for agreeing a change to the service. Including financial data means that the decision is based on much better information so that it is not just on the nature and quality of the service, but also on the cost of each option for the service.

Changes to the service may be identified by the PDCA cycle or triggered by the customer's new business needs. Changes may also be triggered by the service provider's own needs or changes to the circumstances of suppliers. The change to the service may also require a change to the service management processes. Whatever the cause of the change, ISO/IEC 20000-1 requires changes to be costed. ISO/IEC 20000-1 also requires the change to be approved through the change management process. This is described in BIP 0035, *Enabling change.*

CHAPTER 9

Interfaces to other service management processes

Introduction

Budgeting and accounting are both very dependent on information from the other processes, which are in turn also dependent on the quality of information from financial management.

If financial management is seen only as 'something the accountants do' and not as an integral part of service management, information will probably be inadequate or unsuitable as the basis of informed decision making and the whole of service management will suffer. Also, the service management processes are unlikely to be properly integrated, with each service management process operating in isolation.

Implications for integrated service management

Some of the greatest risks arise from a lack of understanding of the importance of financial management being integrated with the other service management processes. Financial management processes play a key role in enabling a service provider to measure value for money of overall service management and of individual processes.

An example of bad practice is service or workload information being provided too late for a budget cycle meaning the budget is unrealistic, impacting the accounting process and ability to provide the service. Similarly, poor quality financial processes can undermine other processes, as described in the following section.

Most service management budgets rely heavily on asset and inventory records being accurate and up to date. For example, the number of PCs is related to the cost of support so if the records are out of date or simply wrong the budget for the cost of support will be wrong.

Another common example of bad practice is the incident management process not recording all incidents and therefore providing a false basis for predicting the impact of a change to the service. At the other extreme the PDCA cycle may accept or reject options for improvements because of incorrect financial information, so that decisions on service improvements are made on the basis of incorrect information. The PDCA cycle and interfaces between service management processes are described in BIP 0038, *Integrated service management.*

Relationships to other service management processes

Typical examples of interdependencies are as follows.

Changes to service
Proposals for new or changed services should consider the cost impact. Associated implementation plans should also be costed.

Configuration management
The service provider needs to define the interface between configuration management and the financial asset accounting processes because financial management requires asset and cost information managed by the configuration management process.

Business relationship management and service level management
These processes work closely with financial management during negotiation of budgets. Service level management works closely with financial management to identify the true costs of service and this information is used for costing options and during the definition, approval and negotiation of new and changed services.

Chapter 10

Example metrics and audit evidence

Metrics used by or provided by financial processes will vary from organization to organization. Examples are included in this chapter, as illustrations, and are neither compulsory for ISO/IEC 20000, nor necessarily comprehensive. Details of the role of metrics are also available in individual books in the 'Achieving ISO/IEC 20000' series, including BIP 0032, *Making metrics work.*

ISO/IEC 20000-1, 3.2 specifies the requirements on audit evidence. A service provider aiming to achieve ISO/IEC 20000 may need to consider audit evidence as part of their service improvement programme. To help understand the type of information that an auditor may seek examples are given in Tables 2 and 3, though these examples are illustrations and not generic requirements.

Table 2 – Example metrics

Metric	Type of Metric	Purpose and ISO/IEC 20000 objectives
Budgets met	Number and percent of budgets met	Costs budgeted in sufficient detail to enable effective financial control
Workload volumes and predicted costs	Numbers of tasks or transactions etc. with any relevant frequency information, e.g. peaks, seasonal trends, previous max/min values, trend information on costs and predicted impact on costs	Budgeting takes into account factors such as seasonal variations
Changes with cost impact	Number and types of change that record estimated costs	Changes to services **shall** be costed

Table 2 – Example metrics (continued)

Metric	Type of Metric	Purpose and ISO/IEC 20000 objectives
Cost comparison data	For example: Cost per device/device type Cost of service per user Cost of service by department/location Unit cost of incident resolution at 1st, 2nd, 3rd line Actual service provider costs as a percent of total organization expenses	Decisions about service provision **should** be based on cost effectiveness comparisons.
Financial improvements	Reduction in budget variances and adjustments	PDCA

Table 3 – Example audit evidence for requirements

Objective and requirement	Example audit evidence
Costs **shall** be budgeted in sufficient detail to enable effective financial control and decision making	• Relevant policy • Process and procedure • Responsibility matrices • Cost types and definition • Cost model • Financial decisions based on financial reports that are related to budgets
The service provider **shall** monitor and report costs against the budget, review the financial forecasts and manage costs accordingly	• Reports of expenditure against budget • Financial trends and forecasts, e.g. by service, by customer, by business unit, by location • Actions from review meetings that demonstrate costs are managed
Changes to services **shall** be costed and approved through the change management process	• Costed options for changes to service referenced from change request • Approval for changes based on impact assessment of costs to the service

CHAPTER 11

Regulatory and legal compliance

Introduction

An audit is completely separate from a financial audit. The former seeks evidence of the quality and effectiveness of processes, whilst the latter is defined by regulatory and legal requirements which are separate from those in ISO/IEC 20000. The requirement for financial processes from a service management perspective might differ from the requirements to produce a true and fair set of accounts for external purposes, such as filing reports under national legislation. However, many of the requirements are linked, overlap or are identical in both types of audit.

Financial policies, processes, procedures and controls are needed to manage financial risk, to ensure control processes are effective, and to minimize fraud. Much of the current legislation affecting service providers has been put in place as the result of high-profile failures in financial controls.

Regulatory and legal compliance is therefore an important business need. This business need is driven by risks ranging from failure to agree company accounts, being forced to suspend trading and prosecution of the organization's senior management. Most organizations have to follow a compliance framework that provides a set of rules for their financial processes that means that all organizations to which the rules apply do their accounting in the same way.

This allows valid comparisons to be made across organizations on their respective financial status. Long-established regulatory requirements are based on accounting standards, company law and principles for financial reporting. Requirements vary from country to country and from sector to sector but most are underpinned by the discipline and control achieved by service management processes for regulation of their technology-based services.

Most regulatory frameworks require a degree of transparency in the accounting process. In some cases there is a requirement for a degree of equity to be adhered to, for instance there are some financial products where the organization is only allowed to keep a specified percentage profit from invested funds. This means it is very important to understand and account for the cost of IT and IT services used in the support of those products. If this is not done there is the risk of penalties such as being fined for retaining funds that should be passed back to investors.

Other examples include European Union laws governing the transfer of prices charged between companies within a group, which are also worth mentioning in connection with the need to maintain costing records. This is because transfer pricing rules in certain situations enable tax authorities to levy tax where they feel that below market rate inter-group agreements have been established. So, for example, where one member of a group provides services to a related company at a price that it could argue is less than that payable under a true 'arm's length' price, EU tax authorities have powers to investigate and require justification of the true cost of the service provision.

Regulatory compliance is separate from achieving compliance with ISO/IEC 20000, but achieving ISO/IEC 20000 delivers greater control and reduced operational risk that supports achieving regulatory compliance. This has increased awareness of service management best practices in many organizations and has for some been the trigger for implementing the full range of service management best practices.

It is not normally necessary for those involved in service management to have knowledge of accounting frameworks in any detail. Instead, service managers (like most parts of an organization) operate under the management direction offered by financial policies, as described in Chapter 3.

Example regulatory compliance requirements

In recent years, new regulatory requirements have arisen, such as those from the European Union and those from the USA. Regulatory frameworks are increasingly being agreed as at least multinational and in some cases international standards for accounting.

For example, one high profile regulatory requirement that has had an impact on many organizations is known as 'Sarbanes Oxley' and is based on the Sarbanes-Oxley Act legislation passed by the USA Government. This affects organizations within the USA, but also many that operate outside the USA who have financial links with the USA.

Regulatory requirements such as Sarbanes-Oxley impose requirements for corporate governance, such that it is now understood that organizations that are required to meet many regulatory requirements find there are substantial benefits from the introduction of best practice processes for the management of IT services and technology-enabled services. This includes drawing on the controls from service management in general, not just the IT budgeting and accounting processes described in this publication.

The impact of these regulations on the service provider is mainly on the controls it needs to operate to ensure the financial systems of the organization as a whole are trustworthy, for instance by ensuring that they are contractually supported, tested and under strong change and configuration controls.

At the core of regulatory frameworks is a requirement that the content of financial information must be relevant and reliable, and that the reporting of financial information must be comparable and understandable. The expectation is that financial information that meets the requirements is of good quality and the information is not confused by inclusion of irrelevant details.

In common with other regulatory or compliance frameworks, Sarbanes Oxley requires:

- clear identification of chargeable items, which are both predictable and measurable;
- a system that enables cost effectiveness to be measured;
- reporting on the variance of forecast and actual costs;
- regular review of the job costing (e.g. cost of setting up a new user);
- charging and billing should encourage the proper usage of computer resources;
- charging and billing should be equitable and reflect the cost of providing the service (e.g. it would be inequitable to charge an additional service for which IT only incurs marginal costs – such as an extra hour on the online day – at a premium rate).

It is also necessary to have good change and configuration management processes so that there is positive assurance that a system can be trusted.

APPENDIX A

ISO/IEC 20000 requirements in summary

It is important to refer to ISO/IEC 20000-1 and ISO/IEC 20000-2 and not rely on the abstract given here, which only covers those parts of ISO/IEC 20000 that are particularly pertinent to financial processes. Other publications in the 'Achieving ISO/IEC 20000' series feature similar tables covering other requirements in the same way.

Each requirement (signified by the use of the verb '**shall**') is supplemented by informative commentary based on the details in ISO/IEC 20000-2 and related publications (see Appendix B). Table A.1 summarizes much of the detail in this publication.

There is only one clause and four requirements directly relating to financial matters in ISO/IEC 20000-1. This apparent simplicity is in contrast to the importance of financial processes in effective service management. However well-designed, implemented and managed a process might be, it may well still not be considered value for money. Very often service managers struggle with understanding costs, budgeting and, where they charge directly for services, charging. To meet the requirements of ISO/IEC 20000 it is essential to have an understanding of costs and how budgets are produced and managed. This is only the minimum for effective service management.

Table A.1 – ISO/IEC 20000 requirements and recommendations with informative commentary/guidance

ISO/IEC 20000-1 requirements	ISO/IEC 20000-2 recommendations (*italics*) and additional commentary (**bold**)
Clause 6.4 *Objective: To budget and account for the cost of service provision.*	
NOTE[7] This section covers budgeting and accounting for IT services. In practice, many service providers will be involved in charging for such services.	*This section covers budgeting and accounting for IT services. In practice, many service providers will be involved in charging for such services.*
However, since charging is an optional activity, it is not covered by the standard.	*However, since charging is an optional activity, it is not covered by the standard.*
Service providers are recommended that where charging is in use, the mechanism for doing so is fully defined and understood by all parties. All accounting practices in use **should** be aligned to the wider accountancy practices of the service provider's organization.	*Service providers are recommended that where charging is in use, the mechanism for doing so is fully defined and understood by all parties.* **It is advisable to plan communications on this well in advance of a new budget being agreed, short notice changes to charging (especially when charging is introduced for the first time) will only succeed if they not only have senior management backing, but new charges are reflected in the new budgets. A generic communication plan that may assist in explaining the reasons for charging and how charges are calculated are described in BIP 0031, *Why people matter*. Failure to explain and justify charges can become a serious overhead to other processes, particularly business relationship management, as described in BIP 0033, *Managing end-to-end services*.**

[7] The NOTE in ISO/IEC 20000-1 is included in the requirements column as it is part of ISO/IEC 20000-1. However, it is not a requirement as it is a NOTE, which either adds an explanation or provides a recommendation. The NOTE provides advice only does text in Part 2.

ISO/IEC 20000-1 requirements	ISO/IEC 20000-2 recommendations (*italics*) and additional commentary (**bold**)
	Responsibility for many of the financial decisions will lie outside the sphere of the service management arena and the requirements for what financial information is to be provided, in what form and at what frequencies may be dictated from outside. **(i.e. outside the service provider's own area of direct authority).** *The provisions of this section are focused on the practices that* **should** *be followed to satisfy the requirements of the standard.* *However, wider requirements* **should** *also be taken into account, as they will impact on some of the policies and procedures defined.* *All accounting practices used* **should** *be aligned to the wider accountancy practices of the whole of the service provider's organization.* **For some aspects of financial processes, particularly those that are related to compliance or regulatory requirements, there may be no option for the service provider to align with the wider accountancy practices of the organization. Even when there is the option, this recommendation is made because the alignment will be beneficial. The alignment with organization-wide accountancy practices does not remove the need for the service provider's financial management to be included in the audit and for them to meet the requirements of ISO/IEC 20000-1 nor should alignment be a barrier to achieving ISO/IEC 20000.**

ISO/IEC 20000-1 requirements	ISO/IEC 20000-2 recommendations (*italics*) and additional commentary (**bold**)
There <u>**shall**</u> be clear policies and processes for:'	***Policy*** *There <u>**should**</u> be a policy on the financial management of services. The policy should define the objectives to be met by budgeting and accounting.* **The ISO/IEC 20000-1 requirement for policies and processes (rather than a requirement for all three of policies, processes and procedures) does not mean that a service provider should ignore the need for financial procedures in the policy, process and procedure hierarchy, only that the auditor may not assess financial procedures but will assess the quality of the policy (or policies) and processes.** **ISO/IEC 20000 requirements will be met with processes that support the policies.**
a) budgeting, and accounting for all components including IT assets, shared resources, overheads, externally supplied service, people, insurance and licences; b) apportioning indirect costs and allocating direct costs; c) effective financial control and authorization.	*The policy <u>**should**</u> also define the detail to which budgeting and accounting are performed, taking into consideration the:* a) *cost types to be accounted for;* b) *apportionment of overhead costs, e.g. flat rate, fixed percentage, or based on the size of the variable element;* c) *granularity of the customer's business e.g. business unit as one unit, subdivided into department, or by locations;* d) *rules governing the handling of variances against budgets, e.g. size of variance that will be escalated to senior management;* e) *links to service level management.*

ISO/IEC 20000-1 requirements	ISO/IEC 20000-2 recommendations (*italics*) and additional commentary (**bold**)
	Each service provider should understand the needs of their customers and suppliers for financial information, not just consider their own parochial interests. **Bullet c) refers to the customer's business because it is advisable to take into account the customer's organizational structure when designing budgeting and accounting, as this can assist with understanding value for money and the relationship between workloads and costs. Also, if charges are levied they ought to be linked to the customer's need for charging information at an appropriate level of detail, i.e. suitably granular when compared to the customers organizational structure, size and scope of individual departments and business functions.** **It is also important that a service provider understands the needs of service management for financial information, and not consider only the need to have information for regulatory and legal compliance.** **The importance of financial information in the PDCA cycle should also be taken into consideration. Many decisions arising from the PDCA cycle cannot be made without sensible and reliable cost information.**
Costs **shall** be budgeted in sufficient detail to enable effective financial control and decision-making.	*The level of investment in budgeting and accounting processes* **should** *be based on the needs of the customers, service provider and suppliers for financial detail as defined in the policy.* *NOTE Service providers operating in a commercial environment might need to invest considerably more time and effort in their financial management.*

ISO/IEC 20000-1 requirements	ISO/IEC 20000-2 recommendations (*italics*) and additional commentary (**bold**)
	Conversely, for service providers where simple identification of costs is sufficient the financial management can be much simpler. *Budgeting and accounting* **should** *be performed by all service providers, whatever their other policies on financial management.* **This is not just a requirement of ISO/IEC 20000, it is also required for legal and regulatory purposes as part of an overall system of internal control to ensure that shareholders and other stakeholders are protected. In addition, UK public sector organizations are normally subject to a requirement to provide Value For Money.**
The service provider **shall** monitor and report costs against the budget, review the financial forecasts and manage costs accordingly.	***Budgeting*** *Budgeting* **should** *take into account the planned changes to services during the budget period and where budgetary requirements exceed available funds, plan for the management of shortfalls.* *Budgeting may take into account factors such as seasonal variations and short- term planned changes to service costs and charges.* *Cost tracking against the budget* **should** *provide early warning of variances against budgets.* *There* **should** *be a process that manages the implications of variances against budget.* *Budgeting and cost tracking* **should** *support planning to operate and change the services so that service levels can be maintained throughout the year.*

ISO/IEC 20000-1 requirements	ISO/IEC 20000-2 recommendations (*italics*) and additional commentary (**bold**)
	Accounting *Accounting processes* **should** *be used to track costs to an agreed level of detail over an agreed period of time.* *Decisions about service provision* **should** *be based on cost effectiveness comparisons.* *Cost models* **should** *be able to demonstrate the costs of service provision.* *Accounts* **should** *demonstrate over- and under-spending/recovery; and* **should** *allow the reader to understand the costs of low service levels or loss of service.* **The ISO/IEC 20000 audit will assess how well the service provider manages actual costs against budgets, not only how the budgets are put in place.** **The integrated approach to service management, required by ISO/IEC 20000 also means the audit will encompass the use of cost information (and charges when applied) in all other service management processes as well as the PDCA, i.e. the requirements are not isolated in the financial aspects of service management.**
Changes to services **shall** be costed and approved through the change management process.	**This is one of the key interfaces between financial processes and the rest of the service management processes as well as the PDCA cycle. More details on interfaces are provided in the other publications in the 'Achieving ISO/IEC 20000' series, but in particular in BIP 0038, *Integrated service management*.**

APPENDIX B

Bibliography and further information

Standards

BS 0-3, *A standard for standards — Part 3: Specification for structure, drafting and presentation*

ISO/IEC Directives Part 2, *Rules for the structure and drafting of International Standards*

ISO 9000, *Quality management systems — Fundamentals and vocabulary*

ISO 9001, *Quality management systems — Requirements*

ISO/IEC 17799, *Information technology — Security techniques — Code of practice for information security management*

ISO/IEC 20000-1, *Information technology — Service management — Part 1: Specification*

ISO/IEC 20000-2, *Information technology — Service management — Part 2: Code of practice*

ISO/IEC 27001, *Information technology — Security techniques — Information security management systems — Requirements*

BSI books

BIP 0005, *A manager's guide to service management*

BIP 0015, *IT service management — Self-assessment workbook*

BIP 0008, *Code of practice for legal admissibility and evidential weight of information stored electronically*

PAS 56, *Guide to business continuity management*

Security information

BIP 0070, *Information security compilation on CD-ROM*

BIP 0071, *Guidelines on requirements and preparation for certification based on ISO/IEC 27001*

BIP 0072, *Are you ready for an ISMS audit based on ISO/IEC 27001?*

BIP 0073, *Guide to the implementation and auditing of ISMS controls based on ISO/IEC 27001*

BIP 0074, *Measuring the effectiveness of your ISMS implementations based on ISO/IEC 27001*

Other resources

British Computer Society: www.bcs.org.uk

British Computer Society Configuration Management Specialist Group: www.bcs-cmsg.org.uk

The IT Service Management Forum (itSMF): www.itsmf.com

EXIN: www.exin.nl

Information Systems Examinations Board (ISEB): www.bcs.org.uk/iseb

The Office of Government Commerce: www.ogc.gov.uk

IT Infrastructure Library (ITIL): www.itil.co.uk

Books in the 'Achieving ISO/IEC 20000' series

There are ten books in the 'Achieving ISO/IEC 20000' series. Each book in the series includes an abstract of ISO/IEC 20000 that is most relevant to the topic of the book, as well as useful contacts and sources of supporting information. These books can be purchased through the BSI website at http://eshop.bsi-global.com.

BIP 0030, *Management decisions and documentation*

This book covers: the background to ISO/IEC 20000; a comparison to other standards and best practice material; compliance and certification audits; the scope of service management; building the business case for achieving ISO/IEC 20000; preparation for an audit and using ISO/IEC 20000 to select your supplier. Important terms that are used in management system standards, where the exact meaning of terms is important to the correct interpretation of the standard, are also explained, including the differences between the terms '**shall**', '**should**' and notes. This book also covers the requirements and recommendations for documents and records, which is a management responsibility requirement in clause 3.2 of ISO/IEC 20000-1.

BIP 0031, *Why people matter*

This book covers the roles and responsibilities of management and process owners, and explains the importance of management commitment to best practice service management, mapping onto the requirements and recommendations of clause 3.1 of ISO/IEC 20000, *Management responsibility*. The book also covers the importance of motivation, training and career development as well as tips and techniques, mapping onto the requirements of clause 3.3 of ISO/IEC 20000-1, *Competence, awareness and training*.

BIP 0032, *Making metrics work*

This book gives a practical view of why metrics and service reports are so important to the delivery of an effective service and to service improvements. It describes the types, the design, target audiences and documentation of metrics used in the service reporting process, covered by the requirements of clauses 4 and 6.2 of ISO/IEC 20000-1, *Plan-Do-Check-Act (PDCA) cycle* and *Service reporting*. Useful tips, techniques and example metrics are included.

BIP 0033, *Managing end-to-end service*

This book describes the supply chains that are commonly managed by service level management, business relationship management and supplier management, which are the requirements in clauses 6.1 and 7 of ISO/IEC 20000-1. It describes the interfaces between suppliers, the service provider and one or many customers. This book also includes useful tips for aspects of end-to-end service, such as the role of service level agreements (SLAs), service reviews, customer satisfaction and complaints procedures.

BIP 0034, *Finance for service managers*

This book covers *Budgeting and accounting for IT services* based on clause 6.4 of ISO/IEC 20000. It introduces financial terms that may be unfamiliar to service management specialists, which will help with understanding the requirements and recommendations. It also covers the relationship between budgeting, accounting and charging, and outlines the importance of service management processes in regulatory compliance.

BIP 0035, *Enabling change*

This book covers the configuration, change management and release management processes which are contained in clauses 9 and 10 of ISO/IEC 20000. It compares the three processes and describes how they interface with each other, and gives advice on the requirements and recommendations of ISO/IEC 20000, example metrics and audit evidence. This book also includes practical advice on meeting the ISO/IEC 20000 requirements on the roles and responsibilities of those involved.

BIP 0036, *Keeping the service going*

This book covers the service continuity and availability management, incident management and problem management processes, which are contained in clauses 6.3 and 8 of ISO/IEC 20000. It explains the role of these processes in keeping the customer's service going, ranging from continuity planning through to the fast-fixing of incidents. It compares the processes and describes how they interface with each other. It includes example metrics and audit evidence, with practical tips and techniques that will help a service provider achieve the requirements.

BIP 0037, *Capacity management*

This book covers the requirements for the capacity management process in clause 6.5 of ISO/IEC 20000. It describes the capacity management process and its role as a link between business plans, workloads, capacity and performance). It also covers the planning required to ensure a service provider is able to deliver a service that allows the customer's business to operate effectively. The book describes capacity management for all types of resources within the scope of service management.

BIP 0038, *Integrated service management*

The opening paragraph of ISO/IEC 20000-1 states that '*This standard promotes the adoption of an integrated process approach to effectively deliver managed services to meet the business and customer requirements*'. This book reflects the importance placed by ISO/IEC 20000 on understanding the interfaces between processes, and how the interfaces are managed so that service management processes are fully integrated. It also reflects the top-down management system approach that is fundamental to ISO/IEC 20000. This book describes how understanding and meeting the requirements of ISO/IEC 20000 gives better control, greater efficiency and opportunities for improvements.

BIP 0039, *The differences between BS 15000 and ISO/IEC 20000*

This book will be of particular interest to those who have used BS 15000 for service improvements, audits or training and need to update their material to reflect the ISO/IEC 20000 standard. ISO/IEC 20000 was based on BS 15000, and this book provides a detailed comparison of ISO/IEC 20000 and BS 15000, for both Parts 1 and 2. It shows the differences in structure, clause numbering and references. The core of this book is a series of tables detailing the changes to the requirements and recommendations clause-by-clause, as well as any re-wording that has been provided to give clarification for an international audience. It includes an explanation of why the changes were made and the implications of each of the changes. This book is based on the material produced by the Project Editor during the drafting of both Parts 1 and 2 of ISO/IEC 20000.